Happiness Is Being
a Physically Fit Christian

HAPPINESS IS BEING A PHYSICALLY FIT CHRISTIAN

Dick Couey

Illustrations by David Guinn

BROADMAN PRESS
Nashville, Tennessee

4275-25

ISBN: 0-8054-7525-7

Dewey Decimal Classification: 613.7

Subject Heading: PHYSICAL FITNESS

Library of Congress Catalog Card Number: 84-12746

Printed in the United States of America

Library of Congress Cataloging in Publication Data

Couey, Dick, 1941-
    Happiness is being a physically fit Christian.

    Bibliography: p.
    1. Physical fitness—Religious aspects—Christianity.
2. Christian life—1960- . 3. Happiness.
I. Title.
BV4598.C68 1985   613.7'0882   84-12746
ISBN 0-8054-7275-7

Dedication

*To Elray, Suzanne, and Paul
whom I truly love*

Fig. 1.1 The total person

Contents

Preface

This book was written primarily for Christians, regardless of age, who are seeking the "abundant life" through serving God to the best of his/her ability. Many Christians are faithful in following God's spiritual directives, but most fail to follow God's directive concerning their responsibility to care for his temple, their body. Many believers are either woefully ignorant or simply negligent toward their bodies. Hopefully, the ideas presented in this book will challenge, motivate, and inspire them to improve their body's physiology in order that they might serve him longer and better. Developing the physical potential that God has given us will help us find that "abundant life," which leads to happiness.

I am grateful to those who have assisted with the book. My sincere thanks goes to my beloved students who served as research subjects. They spent many hours performing exhaustive physical exercises. Appreciation is also extended to my models, Mike Byrd, Duane Knudson, Pam Lowrey, Kay Golson, Carla Belser, and Sharon Hudson, for posing for the pictures.

Special appreciation to David Guinn who did all the artwork. I think he is the best pencil artist in the world. My sincere appreciation to Nancy McGregor for typing my manuscript even though she was swamped with other professors' work.

Finally, my loving and appreciative thanks to Elray, my wife, who sacrificially kept the family together; and to my children, Suzanne and Paul, for their patience and understanding during the long months of study and writing.

CHAPTER 1

Happiness Involves Becoming a Total Person

And Jesus increased in wisdom and stature, and in favour with God and man (Luke 2:52).

Many Christians are frustrated with life. Most are not experiencing the love, joy, and peace, and fulfillment that should be dominant in their lives. Many believers are lonely, some on the verge of hopelessness. Some are suffering from poor health. Some feel that depression is just a way of life. Many ask, "Is this the abundant life that Jesus promised us in John's Gospel?" If you fit into one of these categories, you are not the total person and may be missing happiness.

You ask, "What is a total person?" The definition of a total person does not imply moral or spiritual perfection, nor a state of complete serenity or euphoria, nor a state of perpetual bliss or contentment. It does not mean total fulfillment, though one who is a total person stands a far better chance of being fulfilled. Being a total person does not mean perfection, but it implies being healthy in mind, body, and spirit, and having healthy relationships and attitudes.

It is my belief that a God-inspired discontent within us keeps us feeling unfulfilled and lures us toward a higher degree of becoming a total person. God keeps us seeking, searching, growing until we finally discover the "ultimate." Finding the ultimate, in all probability, will not be attained in this lifetime. That perfection, that ultimate, will be realized only in that heavenly hereafter that we Christians look forward to beyond physical death.

The wholeness that we attain here will be relative rather than ultimate. We can, therefore, define a total person as one who lives in conformity with God's will and standards and is happy to do so. A total person has learned to acquire patience within and toward others. He or she does not expect to receive unconditional love and acceptance all the time. The total person has learned to build up a tolerance for the frustrations and anxieties that besiege every individual. The total person learns to tolerate disappointment, futility, confusion, and occasional failure.

Growth toward becoming a total person involves learning to give, whether it be love, money, encouragement, or time. We soon discover that the very act of giving is a therapeutic or healing factor to our own personalities, as well as in interpersonal relationships. It helps speed our growth toward maturity and wholeness. Jesus realized this important segment of our personality by giving us this beautiful directive, "It is more blessed to give than to receive" (Acts 20:35).

You ask, "How do we develop into a total person?" There was only one person who ever developed into the total person. As we so often do, let us focus our attention on Jesus, examine his life-style, and draw from it perfect examples of how we should live our lives.

In Luke 2:52, the writer summarizes the life of Jesus. From close examination of that Scripture, we can find some revealing hints that can be useful for us in developing into the total person.

This Scripture discloses that Jesus developed in four areas of his life. "And Jesus increased in wisdom [mentally] and stature [physically], and in favour with God [spiritually] and man [socially]." Jesus' development was not only spiritual but also physically, mentally, and socially.

We must realize that God created us and breathed the breath of life into us and we became human beings. As human beings, God gave us freedom to choose how we are going to live our lives. A human being is not just a soul with spiritual needs but a creature of many dimensions. We all have physical, mental, and social needs, and must grow and develop continuously in each area. If we neglect one of these areas, that area will experience decay. This decay will affect other dimensions of our person. We are told in 1 Corinthians 12:26 that "If one part of the body suffers, all the other parts suffer with it" (GNB). Many Christians may be healthy in their spiritual and social needs but unhealthy in their mental and physical selves. The confusions and frustrations caused from being unhealthy in these areas will affect the spiritual and social dimensions. For example, there are many Christians who may have a close relationship with God, or have many friends, but because they become overweight, which often leads to poor health and low self-esteem, lose their enthusiastic desire to continue their spiritual and social development. We must learn to develop our health in all four areas so that we can develop into the total person, just as our Savior did while he lived on this earth some two thousand years ago.

Let us review some ways in which we can develop into the total person, for we have tremendous growth potential in all four areas.

Mental

"And Jesus increased in wisdom." During his life, Jesus demonstrated scholarly growth and development many times.

Fig. 1.2 Mental development

In Luke 2:47, Jesus, at age twelve, amazed even the scholarly priests with his knowledge of Old Testament Scripture. This would have been impossible if he had not spent considerable time in concentrated study of the Scriptures. We should follow the example of Jesus and improve our mental faculties to their fullest potential.

Many Christians in our society fail to cultivate their mental faculties. Watching soap operas on television, reading romance magazines, or attending movies that portray violence and sex is not going to contribute significantly to mental growth.

One rule that must be understood for effective learning is the "overload principle." This principle is basic in developing all four areas of your life. To learn effectively, an overload must be placed consistently on your mental capabilities. This overload should contribute positively, not negatively, to mental development. Read educational books, watch television programs that contribute to your knowledge, and attend lectures or seminars that can broaden your education.

Many Christians have allowed their minds to become stagnant. They go to work, work at the same job every day, return home, and watch the same television programs. They get into the same everyday routine which becomes boring. God has created in the brain tremendous potential for mental development. It is up to you to develop this potential. Do not allow this immeasurable potential to go stagnant. Do not be afraid or too lazy to learn about new areas of life. Develop the God-given potential by consistently overloading your mind with positive educational thoughts. Only when you develop your mental abilities will you become the total person.

Social

"And Jesus increased . . . in favour with man." The overload principle also plays an important part in developing our social skills. God created man with these needs, and he cannot hide from them or neglect them. The Bible tells us that Jesus developed his social needs by attending weddings, religious

Fig. 1.3 Social development

functions, and, on many occasions, dining with friends. Our social needs can be satisfied with positive interpersonal relationships with one another.

In order to establish positive interpersonal relationships you first must be able to learn to love yourself. This doesn't mean loving yourself in a selfish manner. It means you must like the way you are, the way you feel (attitude), the way you think, and the way you behave. If you don't like yourself in these areas, then you will not be able to love others, because they will also conflict with you in these areas. For example, I've known many Christians who became overweight, which caused them to dislike their appearance, which in turn caused emotional conflicts within their personality. They might resent others who are physically fit. This resentment would obviously cause them to lose their witness for him. Jesus understood this when he gave the directive, "you shall love your neighbor as yourself" (Matt. 22:39).

The second thing that you must do in order to improve your interpersonal relationships is to learn how to love everyone. This also includes learning to love the unlovely. Jesus loved every type of person during his time. He loved the rich, the poor, the intellectual, the simpleminded, his friends, and his enemies. We should adhere to his teachings, "but by love serve one another" (Gal. 5:13).

Always be willing to welcome new friends. Seek out people with varied interests, backgrounds, and cultures. Learn and share ideas with these newfound friends. This giving and receiving from the new interpersonal relationships will enhance your social well-being. Only when you make a concentrated effort to make friends will you ever develop into the total person.

Spiritual

"And Jesus increased in . . . favour with God." Jesus learned early in life about the tremendous potential that was given to him for developing a close relationship with God and he spent many hours of his life developing this close relationship with his Father. His growth toward attaining a close relationship with God is one that we should try to duplicate.

Many Christians are unaware of the resources God has provided for leading a rich and exciting life. The untapped potential lies within our grasp, yet we lead a mediocre, roller-coaster existence of occasional mountaintop experiences followed by slides back into the same rut. A few, having never experienced anything else, conclude this must be the normal Christian life. But Jesus came so that believers might have the "abundant" life (John 10:10). Abundant living is not all "peaches-and-cream" experiences. If we are willing to pay the price, God will lead us into fulfillment and adventure with himself. The following principles and guidelines can help us develop our spiritual growth.

Growth Involves Reliance on God's Resources and Personal Effort. The purpose of growing in Christ is to reflect his character to others and to minister to them that they may come to know him. According to the Bible, Christians do not grow just by their own strength but by the actions of God's Spirit within. It is the believer's responsibility to spend time and en-

Fig. 1.4 Jesus was physically fit

ergy fulfilling God's requirements for growth, however (Eph. 4—6).

Frantic efforts to develop spiritual wholeness or a lackadaisical "leave all the rest of God" attitude does not produce growth. We as Christians, are called both to rely on God's resources and to respond in obedience to him.

Live in the Fullness of the Holy Spirit. All who commit their lives to Christ receive the Holy Spirit. However, many Christians still do not yield to him or rely on the resources he brings into their lives. Through ignorance or rebellion, they miss the abundant life Christ promised and enter a cycle of frustration and depression.

If we are to live in the fullness of the Holy Spirit, we must confess all known sin and accept God's cleansing by faith. Confession of all known sin brings cleansing from all unrighteousness, unremembered or unaware as well (John 1:9). This will bring a feeling of peace and freedom to your life.

Another way to live in the fullness of the Holy Spirit is to yield all areas of life to Jesus (Rom. 12:1-2). Many Christians are afraid to totally yield their lives to Christ. They have pet sins they desire to retain. Or, they fear God will cheat them out of a really full life if they submit to him. We must realize that God intends what is best for us (Jer. 29:11). God desires that we spend our lives on things of everlasting value, not on impressive and attractive things the world offers us. If you want to really live life, then yield your life in its entirety to his control, asking him to fill you and take charge. With the help of his power, commit yourself to break with those things displeasing to him and to develop in your life those patterns that honor him.

Grow in Personal Knowledge of God. In order to get to know God you must spend time with him and learn more about him. Develop a daily time with God. Personal relationships demand personal time together. Even Jesus found it necessary to set aside a special time for communication with the Father (Mark 1:35). Our time with God before the day starts will set the tone for all we do that day. Yield to God in prayer for control and filling of your life. Express thanks and praise to him. Pray over matters that will affect you that day.

Gain a practical grasp of God's Word. An understanding of the Bible will help you develop a closer relationship with God. One of the major reasons many Christians do not live a fuller life is that they are ignorant of the Bible's teachings. Unawareness of its guidelines on right and wrong, causes you to fall into sin and waste. Listening, reading, studying, and meditating are excellent methods to achieve a knowledge of God and obedience of his way.

Use Opportunities to Minister to Others. A key part of God's plan for our growth is service. What we receive from him, he desires that we minister to others. We can minister to others about God's grace by becoming a part of a fellowship of Christians. When you join a local church you will have the opportunity to help others and be helped by them, as they teach and encourage you. Learn to share Christ with others around you. If you ask him to, and yield to him, God will use you to share the good news about Christ.

Utilize God's resources (his promises, his Spirit, his Word, and his church) for spiritual growth. Proper use of these resources will help you develop into the total person.

Physical

"And Jesus increased in . . . stature." I picture Jesus as a highly conditioned person. I base my judgment on a study of his life-style. Jesus possessed a high oxygen intake which was evident from the long distances he and his disciples walked. There is evidence that Jesus once walked a distance of 120 miles in a three-day period (Mark 5:6). It would have been impossible to walk those great distances in a short time if Jesus had not been in excellent cardiovascular condition. His day-long journeys often took him up to fifty miles a day through rugged mountainous terrain (Matt. 15:21,29).

In his early life Jesus was a carpenter. His work required him to possess a great amount of strength. He didn't have power tools to aid him, and his tools were not sharpened by power-driven machines. It took strength and muscular endurance just to saw a board. We can see Jesus' strength and condition on the day he was beaten and crucified. Only a well-conditioned man could have survived the beating and torture that preceeded the crucifixion.

This book will be an attempt to explain how Christians should properly care for their bodies, God's temple. Such care will improve the quality of their life and bring happiness. God has created tremendous physical potential in the human body. This physical potential that each person possesses can be reached only through what exercise physiologist describes as the "overload principle." To gain strength or skill, an overload, whether it be a heavy weight or a long practice, must be placed on our present physical ability. The degree of overload will determine the increase in our physical ability. The smaller the overload, the smaller the increase. Conversely, the larger the overload, the larger the increase in physical ability.

This overload must be applied into what exercise physiologist called the "health-related" components of physical fitness. Those areas are cardiovascular-respiratory fitness, body composition, muscular strength and endurance fitness, and flexibility fitness. These health-related components will be discussed in detail in chapters 3, 4, 5, 6, and 7.

CHAPTER 2

Why Should Christians Become Physically Fit?

What? know ye not that your body is the temple of the Holy Ghost which is in you, which ye have of God, and ye are not your own? For ye are bought with a price; therefore glorify God in your body, and in your spirit, which are God's (1 Cor. 6:19-20).

Recently, a church member confronted me after a physical-fitness seminar and asked me this question: Why should Christians become physically fit, for we are only going to use this body for a short time anyway? I tried to answer his question physiologically, but I could see that my answers were not getting through to him. Since that question I have spent much time in prayer and study of the Bible searching for justification of why Christians should become physically fit. Here are some of the reasons I've found.

God's Greatest Creation

The Genesis account of the creation reveals that God's creation of man and woman was his greatest. He created man in his image and likeness (Gen. 1:26), and he breathed the breath of life into his nostrils (Gen. 2:7). The Scriptures disclosed that God was very proud of this creation and remarked, "it was *very* good" (Gen. 1:31, author's italics). Just as we marvel and take pride in things that we do well, so does God marvel and take pride in what he created so perfectly.

Fearfully and Wonderfully Made

One of my favorite Scriptures is found in Psalm 139:13-14. The psalmist was trying to praise God's greatest creation.

You created my inmost being;
  you knit me together in my mother's womb.
I praise you because I am fearfully and wonderfully made (NIV).

Fig. 2.1 "Fearfully and wonderfully made"

As an exercise physiologist, one who studies the functions of the human body as it relates to physical activity, I am amazed at how complicated, how intricate is each part, how diversified is each system, yet how each system lives in such harmony, efficiently performing specific tasks. To me, the human body is perhaps the supreme wonder of the universe.

For example, let us look at some of the marvels of the body as God created it. Let's begin by examining the human cell often called the basic element of life.

The human body begins with the fertilization of a single egg, which is the ultimate wonder among cells. During the next nine months, the egg cell will divide into various types of cells: blood cells, brain cells, nerve cells—almost three trillion cells comprise that clay-colored, wrinkled package of screaming cells we call a baby. A baby is composed of many cells, but is only one organism, and all his three trillion cells know that.

Inside each cell are numerous anatomical structures that regulate the cell's various functions. Each cell has a nucleus that contains the chromosomes responsible for transmitting heredity from generation to generation. With the aid of an electron microscope, examination of the chromosomes reveals that they contain genes, which are responsible for our physical traits such as color of hair or a big nose.

Further magnification of the genes with the microscope reveals that the genes are composed of DNA (deoxyribonucleic acid) and protein. DNA is the substance that binds our cells together. DNA determines how our cellular components behave, what each manufactures, seeks, and avoids. It coordinates the activities of our 100 trillion (number of cells in a 170-pound man) cells as we move, see, think, and feel.

DNA is so narrow and compact that all the genes in our cells would fit into an ice cube; yet when unwound and joined together end to end, the DNA strand would extend from the earth to the sun and back (193 million miles) more than 400 times.

Cells constantly divide and reproduce themselves throughout life. Every second, millions of cells die and millions are formed as old cells divide to create two identical new cells. For example, about two to ten million red blood cells die every second while our body produces one billion each day.

Cells manufacture almost one thousand enzymes, which are remarkable substances. In harmony with RNA (ribonucleic acid) these enzymes, sometimes called master chemists, instantly and effortlessly synthesize proteins. It is estimated that a cell can produce more than one hundred thousand different chemical compounds. A cell can extract protein from digested fish, break it down into its components, and rearrange the amino acids to produce human protein needed for a toenail or another body part.

The number of blood vessels in our body is staggering. If

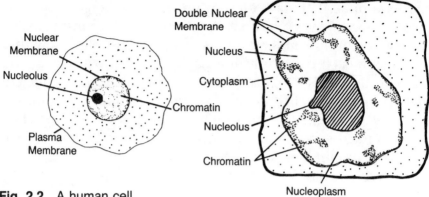

Fig. 2.2 A human cell

we linked all the body's blood vessels together in a 170-pound man, they would extend one hundred thousand miles, or reach four times around the center of the earth.

Perhaps the story of cells can best be summed up by stating that the cell is responsible for everything from the beginning to the end. That 100 trillion cells can live in such harmony, efficiently performing specific tasks, is wonderful to contemplate.

The psalmist expressed himself beautifully when he wrote that we are fearfully and wonderfully made.

God Owns Our Body

God made man in "his own image" and that "man became a living person." The first man was in a state of physical perfection. Every system in his body, including every cell, was in perfect working condition. This was the ultimate in physical fitness. There was no air pollution, noise pollution, junk foods, and automatic, labor-saving devices to mar this perfection. One can almost sense the pride that God felt as he viewed his wonderful creation and served that "it was *very* good" (Gen. 1:31, author's italics).

God knows every minute detail about our bodies. Under the inspiration of the Holy Spirit Paul wrote "What? know ye not that your body is the temple of the Holy Ghost which is in you, which ye have of God, and ye are not your own? For ye are bought with a price: therefore glorify God in your body, and in your spirit, which are God's" (1 Cor. 6:19-20).

This Scripture clearly reveals that your body does not belong to you. Examine this Scripture again. "Know ye not that your body is the temple of the Holy Ghost . . . which ye have of God, and ye are not your own? For ye are bought with a price." God created your body in his likeness, he breathed the breath of life into it, and he paid a great price in proving his love for you and redeeming you from sin. If you are a professing Christian, you have greater reason than others to take care of your body until you take your last breath. For Christians, care of the body is a matter of stewardship. A steward, as defined by Webster, refers to a supervisor who manages an estate or property for someone else. God has given us a body, and he expects us to feed it properly, to rest it properly, to grow in mind and spirit, and to exercise it properly. He wants us to use our body to give glory to him, because he owns it. If we do not keep our bodies in the best possible physical condition, they are incapable of honoring God as they should.

Therefore, as professing Christians and good stewards, we have the responsibility to carefully maintain internally and externally the temples that God created. We should continually and consistently develop our bodies mentally, emotionally, spiritually, and physically for the best possible performance and production capability.

God's Spirit Is in Our Body

God expressed his love for man by giving his son to die for our sins so that those who accept his redeeming love might have eternal life. When we accept Christ, the Holy Spirit comes to live in us. This means, as Christians, our flesh and blood is the earthly dwelling place for the Spirit of God.

> Do you not know that you are God's temple and that God's Spirit dwells in you? If any one destroys God's temple, God will destroy him. For God's temple is holy, and that temple you are (1 Cor. 3:16-17, RSV).

God honors each of us by allowing his Spirit to live within our bodies. What an overwhelming privilege and responsibility we Christians have to house the Spirit of our God. When I think of God dwelling in my body, a sense of responsibility, and feelings of humility and joy fill my mind. I am grateful that God has chosen to live in my body. Knowing that God lives in my body gives me confidence in myself. I am not afraid of taking on life's challenges, for I know God is with and within me. With this feeling of confidence comes a sense of responsibility. I realize that my body will function more effectively and efficiently if I care for its development and maintenance. I am committed to continually and consistently keeping my body at its optimum operating efficiency. This means I must eat properly, rest properly, and exercise properly. It is difficult to understand why some Christians drink alcohol, smoke tobacco, consume harmful drugs, and overeat when the Holy Spirit of God is present within their bodies. It is our Christian responsibility to maintain optimum physical fitness for his temple. When I remember how wonderfully God made his temple and how God expressed his love through his Son, reverence and humility fill my mind. How can God, who created the heavens and earth and breathed life into all life forms, love and honor me by living within my body? All of life's obstacles seem insignificant when compared to the omnipotent presence of God's Spirit within us. The fact that God indwells the body is reason enough to keep our bodies physically fit and a suitable place to show honor and glory to him.

Glorify God in Your Body

Man's option to choose whether he will care for his body and spirit is shown in the last sentence of 1 Corinthians 6:20. "Therefore glorify God in your body and in your spirit, which are God's." God has given man a free will to choose for himself. But he has also given man rules by which to live. God knows that for man to be truly happy he must obey and live his life according to God's directives. Two good examples of God's directives which leads us to happiness are: "You shall love the Lord your God with all your heart, and with all your soul, and with all your mind, and with all your strength" (Mark 12:30, RSV); and learn to "love your neighbor as yourself" (v. 33, RSV). Many Christians who stray from his direction, experience unhappiness from choosing the wrong life-style. We all stray and many of us are still learning to put God first in our life.

In this verse God provides another rule that will contribute to our happiness. He is directing us to glorify God in our bodies to the best of our ability, and to condition our body to its optimum physical capability. If we obey this directive, we will more likely remain healthy throughout our lives. Good health will enhance our service for him and we can serve more effectively without stress and fatigue.

Many Christians choose to neglect this directive. They let false pleasures dominate their bodies. Many overeat, eat foods without nutritional value, drink alcohol, smoke tobacco, worry unnecessarily, and avoid every opportunity to exercise. This life-style is prevalent among Christians of all denominations. This includes many Christians who are obedient to God's spiritual laws; they attend church regularly, tithe, and serve others with compassion and concern, but do not glorify God in their bodies. This lack of obedience to God's command is sin. I feel it is sin to neglect the physical needs of God's temple.

Sins against the body are costly. Our bodies deteriorate from heart disease, high blood pressure, diabetes, and lower back disorders which, in many instances, can be prevented by proper exercise. Christian, you have a choice. You can neglect your body's physical needs, which leads to poor health, or glorify God in your body, which often leads to good health. Your witness to the world and your wellbeing depend on the choice you make.

CHAPTER 3
This Thing Called Fitness

I beseech you therefore, brethren, by the mercies of God, that ye present your bodies a living sacrifice, holy, acceptable unto God, which is your reasonable service (Rom. 12:1).

Recently, a lady asked me this question: "What is physical fitness?" She was confused about what all the literature is saying about running, calisthenics, aerobic dancing, stretching, dieting, and lifting weights. It is easy to understand her confusion for our communication media is flooded with information concerning what you should eat; not eat; how to jog; how to lift weights, etc. Regrettably, most of this information is contradictory and some of it is not based on scientific information. Hopefully, this chapter will help you make a decision concerning your physical fitness needs.

Basically, fitness means being in good physical condition and being able to function at one's best. It is the capability of the heart, blood vessels, lungs, and muscles to function at optimal efficiency. Optimal efficiency means the health needed for the most enthusiastic and pleasurable participation in daily life.

Many fallacies exist about the concept of physical fitness. Some think a physically fit person is the muscular body builder who is capable of knocking down doors or kicking sand in anyone's face if he so desires. Others believe that persons who are slender and can run miles at a fast pace are physically fit; while others believe that a woman who wears a size 6 or 8 dress or a man who has a thirty-inch waist is physically fit. Actually none of these may be classified as physically fit. For example, the muscular person may lack the ability to run a great distance, or the fast person may possess little strength, while the slender person may lack both. Being physically fit

Strength   Flexibility   Cardiovascular-Respiratory Endurance

Fig. 3.1 Health-related components of fitness

encompasses many components. Most exercise physiologists agree that there are ten components of physical fitness. They have divided these components into two categories—health-related and skill-related.

The health-related components are those that best improve the physiological systems of the body, whereas the skill-related components are those essential for performance in games and sports, as well as for working efficiency. The skill-related components will not be discussed here, but they include agility, balance, coordination, power, reaction time, and speed. Having these skills is desirable but is not essential for maintaining a good level of physical health. Your ability to dodge, to control your balance, to react and move quickly, and the ability of your muscles to function harmoniously and efficiently are all reflections of your general athletic skill. This is good news for those who have very limited athletic prowess. You don't have to worry about being chosen last to become fit in the health-related components.

Balance

Coordination

Agility

Speed

Reaction Time

Power

Fig. 3.2 Skill-related components of physical fitness

Health-Related Components

The basic components with health-related fitness are cardiovascular-respiratory (CVR) endurance, body composition, muscular endurance, and flexibility. Each component and its health-related effects on God's temple are discussed below.

CVR Endurance

CVR endurance is the most important health-related component in the fitness area. As its name implies, CVR endurance means becoming fit in the heart, blood, blood vessels, and lungs. Obtaining fitness in these areas reduces the probability of having a cardiovascular disease such as heart attacks and strokes. These circulatory diseases are the leading causes of death among the adult population of most industrialized countries throughout the world. The United States has the unenviable distinction of leading all 168 countries in the world in deaths from these circulatory diseases. Not only do US men lead the men of the world in cardiovascular diseases, but recent statistics show that US women also lead the women of the world in deaths from this disease. In 1982 nearly three million Americans suffered from a cardiovascular disorder, and nearly one million died from one. To illustrate this gruesome statistic, let's suppose that on January 1 an airliner crashed and killed 300 people. Our nation would be in shock over such a tragedy. On January 2 another airliner crashed and 300 more persons perished. The FAA would conduct a serious investigation into the causes and outline possible preventive measures. If on January 3 another airline crashed killing 300 more people, the FAA in all likelihood would completely shut down airports and ground all airplanes until the problem was dealt with. Yet, on the average, 300 people die every day from circulatory diseases and most people in our society don't seem too alarmed.

Americans should be concerned, embarrassed, and ashamed of these statistics because cardiovascular disease can be prevented in most cases. Most exercise physiologists, cardiologists, and other health professionals are convinced that exercise at high enough intensity will improve CVR fitness by either preventing the circulatory disease altogether or by reducing its effects if it does occur. Overwhelming evidence supports the conclusion that exercise reduces the probability of contracting cardiovascular disease. Research has clearly shown that sedentary individuals have a higher incidence of myocardial infarction (heart attack), and that the fatality rate among those who suffer such attacks is higher than in those who are physically active.[1] High levels of CVR fitness lower the serum cholesterol, serum triglycerides, serum glucose, serum uric acid, blood pressure, and body fat percentage. Each of these areas is a risk factor in cardiovascular disease.

Some general and specific recommendations for setting up and carrying out an exercise program to improve CVR fitness are given in chapter 4.

Body Composition

Body composition refers to the relative percentages with fat and fat-free body mass. It is the relative makeup of the body in muscle, fat, bone, and other vital parts. A fit person has a relatively low percentage of body fat.

Obesity in the United States is widespread. Public health records estimate that 50 to 66 percent of Americans are overfat. Forty-six percent are considered obese. Forty percent of our schoolchildren are considered overfat. Retention of body fat is a serious health problem, especially among children and adolescents, because research has shown that the fatty tissue developed at an early age remains throughout a lifetime. This means that fat children often grow up to be fat adults. Life insurance companies claim that overweight individuals are poorer risks than persons with normal weight, as life expectancy is shorter with excessive body fat. The death rate is increased 30 percent for individuals who are 15-24 percent overweight and as much as 80 percent for those who are 35 percent or more overweight.[2]

Diseases of the heart and circulatory system are often associated with obesity. High blood pressure is twice as frequent and arteriosclerosis is three times more frequent in obese individuals. In addition to an increased incidence with coronary heart disease among obese persons, other health problems are manifest. These include diabetes mellitus, gallbladder disease, degenerative arthritis, kidney disease, adverse postural deviations, delayed puberty in children, and decreased endurance and work capacity. Jean Mayer, distinguished professor of nutrition at Harvard, estimates that if all deaths from cancer were eliminated, two years would be added to the human life span; if all deaths related to obesity were removed, the life span would increase seven years.[3] Being overweight is a threat to the quality and length of one's life. The effects of and remedy for obesity are discussed in chapter 5.

Muscular Strength and Endurance

Strength is defined as the capacity of a muscle to exert a maximal force against a resistance. *Muscular endurance* is the capacity of a muscle to exert a force repeatedly over a period of time. In other words, it is the ability to apply strength and sustain it. Even though there is a slight difference between the two, *muscular endurance* and *strength* will be used synonymously.

More and more Americans are beginning to see the need for a good exercise and recreational program. Many are joining recreational programs such as softball, tennis, racquetball, and golf. To be successful in competition, muscular endurance training is necessary. Stronger muscles better protect the bones and joints that they cross. As a result, there is less susceptibility to strains, sprains, fractures, dislocations, and pulls that sometimes occur when playing in sports.

The most important reason for developing muscular endurance is to prevent some of the more common postural deviations that plague the American population such as lower back pain, lordosis, scoliosis, round shoulders, and fallen arches in the feet. Developing muscular balance in all of the major muscle groups will help prevent or rehabilitate most of the postural deviations.

Also many psychological needs are met through toning up flabby muscles. Nearly everyone wants to have the strong lean appearance that can be provided by a good muscular endurance program and a proper diet. A strong healthy body improves one's self-esteen.

We will discuss how to develop a good muscular endurance program in chapter 6.

Flexibility

The fourth important component with health-related fitness is flexibility, which refers to the range of motion possible at a joint or series of joints. In other words, the ability to stretch your muscles and joints. The degree of flexibility depends on ligaments, tendons, and muscles and their extensibility. The bony structures of certain joints place limitations on flexibility, however. Extension of the elbow or knee joint is an example of his limitation.

Even though there are joint limitations, most Christians are far from reaching their flexibility potential. This is evident in the number of Americans with lower back disorders. Loss of flexibility is a common cause of lower back pain. A study of 5,000 patients with back pain revealed that only 20 percent had some underlying structural problem such as damaged vertebrae, herniated disc, or arthritis. The remaining 80 percent were diagnosed as being caused by inelastic or weak muscles.[4] The need to develop both flexibility and strength to prevent lower back problems is obvious.

Flexibility is also important in reducing muscle soreness after vigorous physical exertion. Flexibility helps reduce the chance of incurring torn ligaments or pulled muscles during activity. In summary, individuals with good flexibility have less postural deviations, less stiffness and soreness of muscles, better skill proficiency, and less chance of injury during movement. A flexibility program is described in chapter 7.

Many Christians in America present an example of poor physical fitness. They are rundown and somewhat pudgy. They eat erratically a grossly unbalanced diet, some pollute their body's ventilating system with poisonous gases, some drink alcohol, and many sit before the TV some ten to fifteen times longer then they spend exercising their bodies. Emotionally they fall short of achieving their goal of real peace of mind. Their minds are filled with guilt and frustation. They are unhappy, lonely, and generally dissatisfied with their lot in life. Spiritually, they show little evidence of having a close relationship with God. They suffer from a spiritual depression that robs them of the joy, peace, and satisfaction that are the natural consequences of a spiritually mature Christian.

Is your life described in the above paragraph? If so, maybe you have something missing in your life that keeps you from living up to your potential. Being physically fit plays an intrinsic part in developing into the "total person." If you develop your fitness in each of the health-related components of physical fitness, then you will become a good witness for God which will bring happiness to your life.

Notes

1. Joseph Bonanno, "Effects of Physical Training on Coronary Risk Factors," *American Journal of Cardiology,* 33 (1974), 760.

2. J. Mayer, *A Diet for Living* (New York: Pocket Books, 1977).

3. Ibid.

4. H. F. Farfan, Mechanical Disorders of the Lower Back (Philadelphia: Lea and Febger, 1973).

CHAPTER 4

Happiness Involves Becoming Cardiovascular/ Respiratory Fit

Let us also lay aside every encumbrance, and the sin which so easily entangles us, and let us run with endurance the race that is set before us, fixing our eyes on Jesus, the author and perfecter of faith (Heb. 12:1-2, NASB).

Probably no other component of physical fitness is more important in improving the health and well-being of God's temple than cardiovascular-respiratory (CVR) endurance. As mentioned in chapter 3, CVR endurance means becoming fit in the heart, blood, blood vessels, and lungs. Obtaining fitness in these areas reduces the probability of having a cardiovascular disease such as heart attack, high blood pressure, and strokes.

For example, today a forty-five-year-old man can expect to live only three years longer than his grandfather did in 1900. This seems erroneous because Americans have the best medical technology, the best quality and greatest quantity of food, and the best educational system in the world. It seems inconceivable that we are able to expand our life expectancy only three years. Average overall life expectancy has increased to 74.1 years, but this has been due to a decrease in infant mortality and the control of communicable diseases such as polio, pneumonia, and tuberculosis. The reason Americans have not increased their life expectancy beyond three years is because of the epidemic rise in cardiovascular disease. This disease is beseiging the American population and is not limited to any specific age group.

The most common cardiovascular disease and the underlying cause of many heart attacks and strokes is *atherosclerosis*. Atherosclerosis is a form of arteriosclerosis, characterized by

Table 4.1 Comparison of the Length of Life in U.S. Presidents Before 1900 and After 1900.
(Deaths due to natural causes)

Length of Life for Presidents before 1900
(Death due to natural causes)

Adams	—90 years
Jefferson	—83 years
Madison	—85 years
Monroe	—73 years
J. Q. Adams	—80 years
Jackson	—78 years
Van Buren	—75 years
	81 years (average)

Length of Life for Presidents after 1900
(Death due to natural causes)

T. Roosevelt	—60 years
Wilson	—67 years
Harding	—57 years
Coolidge	—60 years
F. Roosevelt	—78 years
Johnson	—64 years
	64 years (average)

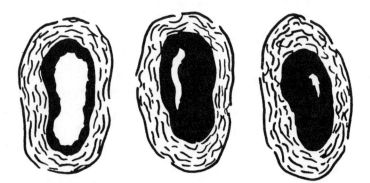

Fig. 4.1 Process of atherosclerosis. Fats stick to sides of artery which reduces blood flow.

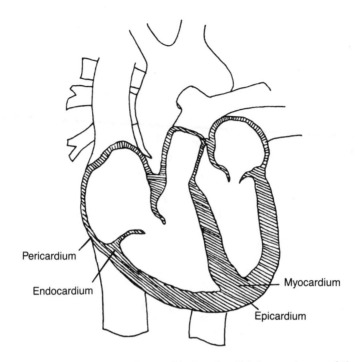

Fig. 4.2 Tissue layers of the heart. Notice the thickness layer of the myocardium.

hardening of the arteries. This disease is usually caused by hyperlipidemia, an increase of fat (lipid) in the blood (fig. 4.1). Cholesterol and triglycerides are the most common lipids associated with atherosclerosis. These lipids collect in the linings of arteries and block blood circulation. A collection in the artery walls anywhere in the circulatory system may cause a blood clot to form. If the clot blocks an artery, that body part (cells) loses its blood supply and usually dies. When this occurs in the artery supplying the heart or brain, a coronary heart attack or stroke results. Formation of a blood clot that results in blockage is called *thrombosis*. Coronary arteries supply the heart muscle, *myocardium* (fig. 4.2), with blood, and blockage of these arteries is called a *coronary thrombosis* or heart attack (fig. 4.3).

Atherosclerosis is not associated primarily with old age. Although it may not be a problem until middle age, it can develop at an early age and affect the entire body. The first indications that atherosclerosis developed in young people came from autopsies performed during the Korean and Vietnam wars. Seventy-seven percent of those men, whose average age was only twenty-one, had marked evidence of fatty deposits in coronary arteries. In two studies of children, ages seven to twelve years, 60 percent exhibited at least one risk factor associated with coronary heart disease in adult populations (obesity, high-serum cholesterol and triglycerides, elevated blood pressure, and low work capacity). These results indicate that we need to develop positive attitudes in children and young adults about the importance of physical fitness as a deterrent to atherosclerosis.

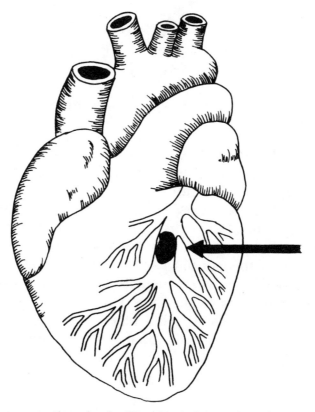

Fig. 4.3 A coronary thrombosis. The blood clot restricts all blood flow to lower portion of the heart.

Atherosclerosis is often called "the aging disease." Blood contains oxygen and nutrients that are essential to the cell. If a cell is denied blood, it will die. If enough of these cells are destroyed, tissues and organs will fail to function efficiently, causing the body to age and deteriorate. To slow this aging disease, we need to consume fewer high cholesterol foods, ingest a diet low in calories, and maintain a high level of physical activity. This will allow a constant flow of blood to all body cells, which will delay the aging processes and enhance our chances of living a healthier and happier life in which to serve our Lord.

Although much needs to be learned about the causes and cures of heart attacks, medical studies have associated certain conditions or living habits with this disease. The most significant study is the Framingham study in which data were collected from 1955 to 1970 from men and women ages thirty to sixty-two. From these data, certain conditions or living habits associated with heart attacks were identified and labeled as risk factors. The presence of only one factor increases the chance of having a heart attack, and combinations of two or more multiply the risk considerably. The following are the most implicated coronary risk factors: (1) elevated blood lipids (fats); (2) hypertension; (3) cigarette smoking; (4) physical inactivity; (5) obesity; (6) tension and stress; (7) heredity; (8) diabetes mellitus; (9) personality and behavior patterns; (10) high uric acid levels; (11) electrocardiographic abnormalities during rest and exercise; (12) diet; (13) pulmonary function abnormalities; (14) alcohol consumption; and (15) age and sex.

The importance of a single risk factor compared with any other is difficult to determine quantitatively because many factors are interrelated. For example, blood lipid abnormalities, diabetes, heredity, and obesity go hand in hand. Elimination or reduction with one or more risk factors may cause a corresponding decrease in the probability of a heart attack. Let's discuss blood lipid abnormalities and physical activity as they have received the greatest public attention.

Cholesterol and triglycerides are the two most common

lipids associated with coronary heart disease. Cholesterol is not a foreign substance, but an important constituent of the body. It is essential for every body organ and is a structural part with the cell wall. It is also found in myelin, a white sheath that surrounds and insulates nerve strands. It helps form bile acids for digestion and produces hormones and essential vitamins. On the negative side, cholesterol may cause gallstones and anemia as well as atherosclerosis.

Some cholesterol is present in foods that come from animal sources. In addition, the liver produces about 600 milligrams of cholesterol daily. Cholesterol from both sources circulates in our bloodstream. Thus even if the diet contains no cholesterol, the body would still produce it. The concentration level of cholesterol in the blood is measured as the number of milligrams in every 100 milliliters of blood. When an individual's cholesterol level is 200 for example, his blood contains 200 milligrams of cholesterol per 100 milliliters.

Cholesterol is found in food that comes from animal sources, such as meats, poultry, eggs, butter, milk, and cheese. There is none in plant foods, such as vegetables, grains, fruits, and nuts. The amount of cholesterol in animal foods varies widely. One large egg yolk (the cholesterol is in the yolk) has about 252 milligrams. Animal organ meats are rich in cholesterol. Beef liver has 372 milligrams in a three-ounce serving, whereas calf brains have a huge 2,668 milligrams. Beef, pork, and processed luncheon meats are fairly high in cholesterol. Shellfish, such as shrimp, clams, oysters, and scallops, have somewhat less. Fish and poultry have less cholesterol than shellfish.

Research has recently found that food is not the main source of cholesterol in the blood. The amount of cholesterol in the bloodstream depends on all the fats you eat. The quantity and type of fat affects cholesterol level. There are three chemical types of fat: saturated, monounsaturated, and polyunsaturated. Saturated fats have carbon atoms filled with hydrogen atoms. Monounsaturated fats contain carbon atoms with additional space for one more hydrogen atom. Polyunsaturated fats contain carbon atoms with two or more available spaces in each hydrogen atom.

Saturated fats occur in animal foods already high in cholesterol, such as beef, ham, pork, butter, whole milk, eggs, and cheese. Eating this type of fat contributes to *increased* blood cholesterol levels. Monounsaturated fats, such as olive oil and peanut oil, have *no* significant effect on cholesterol level. Many researchers believe that polyunsaturated fats, such as corn oil, safflower oil, sesame oil, and soybean oil, *reduce* blood cholesterol. How these three kinds of fats change the blood cholesterol level in different ways is unknown, although the effect presumably is tied to the variations in hydrogen atoms in their molecules.

Studies of the average cholesterol levels of people in various countries show that the higher the country's cholesterol level, the higher its heart attack rate. In comparing men in Japan, Finland, and the US, for example, the Japanese had an average cholesterol level of 140, which is much lower than the world average of 170. They also have the world's lowest heart attack rate for industrialized countries. The Finns have the highest cholesterol level in the world, averaging about 280, and they also have the world's highest heart attack rate (ten times the Japanese rate). The US ranks second to Finland in heart attack occurrence (first in deaths). The cholesterol level for middle-age American men averages 225.

Research has also shown ties between cholesterol levels and saturated fat in each country's diet. The Japanese, with the lowest heart attack rate, ate the lowest amount of saturated fat (about 3 percent of all calories in the diet). The Finns, with the highest heart attack rate, ate the greatest amount of saturated fats, about 20 percent of their total calories, with a record consumption of butter, cheese, milk, and sausage. Americans consume about 18 percent of their total calories in saturated fats. The relationship between cholesterol and saturated fat consumption and heart attacks should be obvious.

A very interesting study done on the Masai (a tribe of East African cattle herders) seems to contradict the diet-heart disease theory. The Masai live primarily on fermented cow's milk, rich in saturated fats and cholesterol, yet a heart attack in their society is virtually nonexistent. One possible reason for this apparent contradiction could be exercise which, according to many studies, lowers the cholesterol level. Masai herdsmen walk an average of twenty-six miles a day. Then, for amusement, compete in games which require them to leap straight up in the air for hours at a time. They are among the healthiest and most physically fit people in the world.

Experts have now uncovered evidence that some types of cholesterol may actually be of value. These findings may dispel the contradictions in the diet theory and are based on new knowledge about all fats in the blood. Scientists have researched the role of triglycerides in atherosclerosis. Triglycerides make up 98-99 percent of the weight of food fats. Neither cholesterol nor triglycerides dissolve in water. These essential compounds in their unaltered form cannot travel in the bloodstream, which consists mainly of water. So these blood fats are linked with proteins to form molecules that are soluble in water. These molecules are called *lipoproteins*.

Lipoproteins fall into four major groups, classified according to density. The lighest pick up triglycerides from foods that contain fats. They consist of up to 95 percent triglycerides, with a small amount of cholesterol.

Next in weight are very low-density lipoproteins. They carry only 15 percent of the cholesterol moving in the blood.

Heavier still are low-density lipoproteins (LDL). These are rich in cholesterol, transporting about 65 percent of the cholesterol in the blood.

Heaviest still are high-density lipoproteins (HDL), which carry only about 20 percent of blood cholesterol.

Researchers found that men with coronary heart disease generally had lower than average HDL levels. Later studies showed that men with the high total cholesterol levels linked to heart disease also had high LDL levels. Apparently LDLs are the major source of the cholesterol deposited in the plagues of atherosclerosis. Research done on six ethnic populations revealed that HDLs protect against heart disease. This means the higher the HDL level, the lower the risk.

One widely accepted theory holds that HDLs act as scavengers, gathering cholesterol from cells and tissues and returning it to the liver. Another theory suggests that HDLs interfere with the absorption of LDL cholesterol within the cells.

Whatever the explanation, the facts are clear. Among the Framingham subjects, for example, the average man had an HDL level of forty-five, whereas the average women had a level of fifty-five. This discrepancy may account for the lower rate of heart attacks in women. Statistical analysis shows that for every five points the HDL level falls below the forty-five mark, the risk of coronary heart disease increases by 25 percent. On the other hand, very high HDL readings seem to indicate longevity. In families with HDL levels over seventy-five, some members live into their ninety's relatively free of atherosclerosis. These high HDL levels are apparently inherited.

In a study done by Dr. Ken Cooper, an authority on aerobic research, he found that the ratio between total cholesterol level and HDL level should be under 4.5 to 1 to afford better protection against heart disease. Dividing the HDL level into the total cholesterol level will determine this ratio. For example, the HDL level was determined to be 60, whereas, the total cholesterol was determined to be 180. The ratio would be 3:1. Personally, I feel Christians should lower this ratio to 3:1 to better protect against heart disease. A simple blood test conducted by a physician can determine your HDL and total cholesterol level.

The question arises; how do you improve HDL level while reducing the total cholesterol level? To improve the ratio of cholesterol to HDL, diet remains important. By eating less cholesterol and saturated fat, you may change the ratio in your favor. It is also important to stop smoking, drinking alcohol, and get regular exercise.

The value of exercise indicates that men who exercise regularly have significant better HDL levels than inactive men.

The HDL level among the Masai men averaged 78. Studies also reveal that sedentary, overweight people can, after participating in exercise programs, improve their HDL levels.

If Americans lowered the cholesterol concentration in their bloodstream by 10 percent, cholesterol would drop twenty points, which would cause the incidence of new coronary heart disease to be lowered by 24 percent. If cholesterol concentrations were lowered by 20 percent, the incidence of coronary disease would be lowered by nearly 50 percent.

If you wish to protect yourself against heart-related disease, the recommended course is simple:

1. Reduce your consumption of foods that come from animal sources. At least, trim all visible fat from beef, pork, and lamb.
2. Eat more fish and veal.
3. Skin poultry and discard the fat.
4. Drink skim milk rather than whole milk.
5. Bake or broil rather than fry.
6. Exercise daily for at least thirty minutes in duration.

The Health Benefits Received from Becoming Cardiovascular-Respiratory Fit

Effects on the Heart

One of the most beneficial long-term effects is an increase in the size and strength of the heart muscle (myocardium) and a high-stroke volume (amount of blood pumped per beat) at all levels of activity. With increased stroke volume, the heart does not have to pump as fast in order to supply the body with a given amount of blood for a particular level of activity. The slower heart rate at all levels of activity, resting and during heavy work, allows the heart more rests between contractions. This slow heart rate is evident in well-trained individuals. Studies done on American Olympic track athletes revealed a resting heart rate in the lower thirties per minute, much slower than for the average American (seventy-two beats per minute for males; eighty beats per minute for females). Simple calculations reveal how much more efficient the heart of a well-trained individual is compared with the average person:

$$
\begin{array}{rl}
70 & \text{beats/minute average American} \\
-40 & \text{beats/minute well trained} \\
\hline
30 & \text{less beats per minute} \\
\times 60 & \text{minutes in hour} \\
\hline
1800 & \text{beats less in one hour} \\
\times 24 & \text{hours in day} \\
\hline
43{,}200 & \text{less beats in one day} \\
\times 365 & \text{days in year} \\
\hline
15{,}768{,}000 & \text{beats less in one year}
\end{array}
$$

The only time the heart rests is between contractions. From these calculations we can determine that a well-trained heart will rest approximately three months longer than an unconditioned heart in a year's time.

In the well-conditioned individual, the heart rate also responds more quickly to various work loads and recovers faster to its normal rate. Because of its ability to supply an adequate amount of blood at a lower heart rate, the heart is able to tolerate greater work loads before reaching its maximum rate. For the average person, this can provide a reserve capacity to cope with sudden physical or emotional stresses that accelerate the heart rate. In a well-trained individual, a substantial amount of vigorous activity over a relatively long period of time is required to raise the heart rate to its maximum. For example, let us imagine that Alberto Salizar (world record holder in the marathon) agreed to run an eight-minute mile with Mr. Average American. If we monitored each person's heart rate during and after the mile run, it would probably reveal that Salizar's heart rate during the run reached approximately 140 beats per minute, whereas Mr. Average American's (if he finished) heart rate approached 200 beats per minute. Both did the same amount of work (ran an eight-minute mile), but the stress of running had different effects on their hearts. Also, probably within five minutes after the mile run, Salizar's heart rate would recover to its normal resting rate, whereas Mr. Average American's heart rate probably would recover in maybe one hour, maybe even days.

Other long-term effects on the heart rate include an increase in the size and elasticity of the coronary arteries and an increase in the size and number of functioning capillaries. Latent ones are opened and new ones are formed. This increased size of the coronary arteries provides greater blood flow under less resistance and can prevent or delay the closing of these arteries caused by accumulation of fatty deposits on the lining. The greater size and number of capillaries provide the heart with more nourishment and with a better distribution of oxygen for its energy needs, thereby increasing efficiency. They also allow for easier removal of waste products and delay the fatigue that waste products buildup can cause. To illustrate these findings, an autopsy performed on Clarence De Mar (a distance runner who averaged running nearly twelve miles a day for fifty years), revealed that his coronary arteries were clear of fatty buildup (atherosclerosis) and that his heart muscle did not show any signs of fibrosis (development of scar tissue from lack of circulation) even though he was seventy years old at his death from cancer.

By increasing the capillary beds, regular exercise also develops collateral circulation in the heart (fig. 4.4). Collateral circulation refers to connection between arteries and veins of the same diameter and between larger and smaller vessels. This is important in continuing or reestablishing circulation when a main vessel is closed off. An autopsy performed on astronaut Ed White (who burned to death in a cabin explosion during a test) showed a complete closing of one major coronary artery from atherosclerosis. Yet, because of a large buildup of collateral circulation, White had been able to function at a high level of physical efficiency.

Effects on the Vascular System

Exercise causes the size and elasticity of the arteries to increase throughout the body as do the size and number of cap-

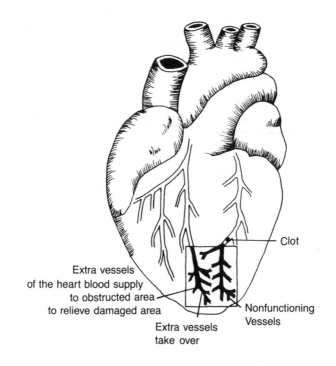

Extra vessels
of the heart blood supply
to obstructed area
to relieve damaged area

Extra vessels
take over

Clot

Nonfunctioning
Vessels

Fig. 4.4 Coronary collateral circulation

illaries in the various tissues. Collateral circulation between all major arteries increases and there is better diffusion between the capillaries and the working tissues. Improved blood flow takes an additional load off the heart. The enlargement and increase in the number of blood vessels decreases resistance to blood flow and lowers an abnormally high blood pressure. The effect also helps blood pressure to return to normal faster following an increase from any cause. By increasing the size and helping to maintain elasticity of the large arteries, hardening of the arteries can be prevented or delayed.

Effects on the Blood

Red blood cells are significantly increased through regular exercise. Studies comparing well-trained with untrained individuals have shown that well-trained individuals have between seven and eight million red blood cells per cubic millimeter of blood, whereas untrained individuals have between five and six million. Because red blood cells combine with oxygen, the well-trained individual is better able to transport more oxygen to the starved cells. Greater oxygen flow to brain cells makes you think and feel better.

Two other beneficial effects relate to the formation of blood clots and the level of fatty acids in the blood. Exercise affects the clotting time of blood in two ways: the blood coagulates more quickly when it leaves the vascular system, such as from a cut, and the blood plasma activity increases, which breaks up blood clots forming within the blood vessel. This lessens the chance of a blood clot forming in the heart, brain, or other vital organs.

Numerous studies have shown that residual levels of cholesterol and other fatty lipids in the blood can be significantly reduced with vigorous exercise. Reducing cholesterol and triglycerides significantly reduces your chance of atherosclerosis. Vigorous exercise also increases high-density lipoprotein (HDL), which reduces atherosclerosis.

The beneficial effects of regular exercise demonstrate why the incidence of cardiovascular disease has consistently been lower in physically active people than in those who lead more sedentary lives. The effects also explain why an increasing number of doctors are prescribing exercise for patients showing signs of degenerative cardiovascular disease and even patients who are recovering from certain types of heart attacks.

How to Develop Cardiovascular Respiratory Fitness

After realizing the need and understanding the benefits of CVR fitness, the question arises, "How can I develop CVR fitness?" I now deal with that question by looking at the intensity, duration, and frequency of exercise.

Intensity

Intensity refers to how stressful an exercise is to the CVR system. Beginners often ask how hard they must exercise in order to develop a training benefit. They want to know at what point in their training they will begin to notice the desirable attributes that accompany CVR conditioning. Everyone wants to know how fast to walk, jog, swim, or exercise for the body to get stronger and improve its health.

The intensity threshold is directly related to one's present level of CVR condition. This means, the more fit one is, the higher the intensity level must be to improve CVR conditioning. Conversely, the less fit one is, the lower the intensity level has to be to improve CVR condition. The best way to measure this intensity threshold would be through determining one's maximum oxygen uptake. This procedure requires the use of specially designed equipment operated by an exercise physiologist. Most individuals do not have the time or money to go through this procedure. Fortunately, exercise physiologists have devised a simpler, but less accurate manner in which to determine one's threshold intensity. This procedure does give one a fairly accurate ball-park estimation.

This procedure requires the knowledge of taking one's pulse rate. Karvonen developed the following formula to determine how fast the heart should beat while exercising in order to produce a training benefit. Examples of persons twenty and forty years of age with a resting heart rate of sixty beats per minute are used.

20-Year-Old Man		40-Year-Old Man
220		220
−20	age	−40
200	maximum heart rate	180
−60	resting heart rate	−60
140		120
×.70	(threshold intensity)	×.70
98.00		84.00
+60	resting heart rate	+60
158	desired working heart rate	144

Thus a twenty year-old person experienced at exercising with a resting heart rate of sixty must train at 158 heartbeats per minute to receive a training benefit. When the heart rate reaches this threshold level, then the body's physiological functions will become more efficient, the heart will beat more slowly while at rest, blood pressure will achieve normalcy, cholesterol and triglycerides will be utilized for energy, and atherosclerosis will be delayed.

To determine your maximal heart rate, subtract your age from 220. Determine your resting heart rate by first sitting down for fifteen minutes of quiet rest or take it when you first wake up in the morning. At the end of this rest period, count your pulse for one minute. Subtract your resting heart rate from your maximum heart rate. Multiply this difference by 70 percent if you have been exercising consistently. If you have not exercised in months then multiply this difference by 60 percent. Also if you are over fifty years of age, use the 60 percent intensity level, especially if you were inactive in your earlier years. Now add your resting heart rate to get the working heart rate at which you should train.

Ways of exercising to elevate the heartbeat to a desirable threshold intensity include walking briskly, jogging, swimming, bicycle riding, or playing a vigorous game such as tennis or racquetball. To determine the desired intensity or rate of your heart beat, record your pulse beat immediately after exercising for four or five minutes. If your heart rate is below the desired rate, then speed up your method of exercise. You may need to walk or jog a little faster to cause your heart rate to rise with increased intensity until it reaches a steady state condition (a condition in which the heart rate can supply enough oxygen to the muscles so they can create enough energy to do the exercise work without an increase in heart rate). If your heart rate is higher than the threshold intensity, you may want to slow down your exercise pace. Slowing down is unnecessary if you desire to increase your CVR fitness to a higher degree. Remember, the higher the intensity, the greater the increase in CVR endurance.

Before beginning a cardiovascular training program, heed these precautions. If you are just beginning an exercise program, or if you have not exercised within the past four weeks, start the program below the suggested threshold rate of 70 or 60 percent. Depending on age and present physical condition, it is advisable to begin at the 40 percent intensity level. Substituting the 40 percent intensity level in the forty-year-old person's example reveals the threshold intensity heart rate to be 108 beats per minute. Slowly allow the CVR system to build itself up to handle the more vigorous stress. Beginning at a low intensity level also helps the muscles, tendons, and ligaments build up their strength to properly handle the stress of exercise. This alleviates pulled or strained muscles that could occur in exercising. Do not try to do too much in a short time; go slowly and gradually increase your intensity level. You have the rest of your life to obtain your optimum fitness level.

Duration

The duration of an exercise session is important in improving the cardiovascular functions in the body. Recommended times vary from five to thirty minutes. From personal experience and research, my conclusion is that the duration of an exercise session should be proportionate to your present level of cardiovascular fitness. If you are highly fit, you should exercise longer. This longer duration increases your cardiovascular fitness to your optimum level. Conversely, if your fitness is low, you should exercise for a shorter time, or until you are able to slowly, progressively increase your time. As you get stronger, you can safely increase your duration without unduly stressing your cardiovascular system. Research done on duration and its effect on HDL development revealed that a significant increase session exceeded thirty minutes. Depending on your present fitness level, try to exercise for approximately thirty minutes at your heart rate threshold level.

Frequency

Determining the necessary frequency of exercise is also important. Some of the fitness literature claims that exercising one day each week is ideal in obtaining the optimum level of

CVR fitness. In my opinion, if you acquire the urge to exercise once or twice a week, you should go and lie down until that urge passes. It is more harmful to exercise once or twice a week than not to exercise at all. Infrequent exercising can cause stress to the CVR system, which is incapable of handling the severe increase in heart rate, blood pressure, oxygen intake, and respiration that occurs from vigorous exercise.

The key to safe exercising is to develop consistency. Make an effort to exercise at least three times a week, preferably four to six times. Find a specific time of day for exercising (preferably after your working hours) and stick to it. Guard this precious time from any outside interference. Avoid gaps of more than forty-eight hours between exercise sessions. Research has shown that circulating blood levels of triglycerides and cholesterol, even though reduced by exercise, return to higher levels within forty-eight hours unless exercise is repeated.

The type of exercise used in these training sessions is relatively unimportant as long as the preceding criteria are met. Walking, jogging, skiing, bicycling, swimming, rope skipping, aerobic dancing, roller skating, rowing, and stair climbing are all excellent. Various sport activities that require running also can be beneficial—basketball, racquetball, handball, tennis, and badminton. Variety will keep your interest in the exercise program. Jogging, swimming, skiing, aerobic dancing, and bicycling are perhaps the best all-around activities for CVR conditioning because they require a high percentage of aerobic energy output. Participation in a sport may take longer to gain the same CVR training effects but is satisfactory if that is your choice.

How to Evaluate Your Present Level of CVR Fitness

Before beginning a CVR training program, your present physical condition should be assessed in comparison to established standards of fitness. This will help you to better plan the type of program needed. You may even want to repeat this assessment at periodic intervals to chart progress.

The best measurement of CVR fitness is maximum oxygen consumption. This is the maximum amount of oxygen that the body can consume while working at its higher level of intensity. The body takes oxygen and changes it into energy called adenosine triphosphate (ATP). This means a fit person can do more work than an unfit person because of the extra energy created.

Accurate measurement of maximum oxygen consumption requires time-consuming laboratory procedures done by specialists in exercise physiology. Fortunately, valid short-cut procedures that provide rapid and inexpensive methods for determining CVR fitness level have been devised. The Cooper one and one-half mile test is probably the simplest to take while providing an accurate measurement of maximum oxygen uptake.

Cooper's One and One-Half Mile Run Test

To evaluate your CVR fitness, run or walk a flat, accurately measured distance of one and one-half miles as fast as possible and record your time with an accurate watch to the nearest second. Compare your fitness with others in your age group (table 4.2).

The one and a half mile test gives a fairly accurate determination of CVR fitness despite some error of determination due to individual differences and motivation to do one's best. All Christians should strive to obtain the excellent to superior rating which would improve their health benefits and show honor to God with their body.

Some Programs for Developing CVR Fitness

CVR fitness can be developed from a variety of activities, but the amount of increase and the speed in which fitness is obtained depend on the principles of intensity, duration, and frequency. A good rule of thumb is the higher the intensity, the less the duration. Conversely, the lower the intensity, the longer the duration, provided that frequency of the activity re-

Table 4.2 1½ Mile Test for Men and Women

Fitness Category	13-19 Men	13-19 Women	20-29 Men	20-29 Women	30-39 Men	30-39 Women	40-49 Men	40-49 Women	50-59 Men	50-59 Women	60+ Men	60+ Women
Very Poor	15:31+ (min.)	18:31+	16:01+	19:01+	16:31+	19:31+	17:31+	20:01+	19:01+	20:31+	20:01+	21:01+
O₂ Uptake ML/Kg/min.	<35.0	<25.0	<33.0	<23.6	<31.5	<22.8	<30.2	<21.0	<26.1	<20.2	<20.5	<17.5
Poor	12:11-15:30 (min.)	16:55-18:30	14:01-16:00	18:31-19:00	14:44-16:30	19:01-19:30	15:36-17:30	19:31-20:00	17:01-19:00	20:01-20:30	19:01-20:00	20:31-21:00
O₂ Uptake ML/Kg/min.	35.0-38.3	25.0-30.9	33.0-36.4	23.6-28.9	31.5-35.4	22.8-26.9	30.2-33.5	21.0-24.4	26.1-30.9	20.2-22.7	20.5-26.0	17.5-20.1
Fair	10:49-12:10 (min.)	14:31-16:54	12:01-14:00	15:55-18:30	12:31-14:45	16:31-19:00	13:01-15:35	17:31-19:30	14:31-17:00	19:01-20:00	16:16-19:00	19:31-20:30
O₂ Uptake ML/Kg/min.	38.4-45.1	31.0-34.9	36.5-42.4	29.0-32.9	35.5-40.9	27.0-31.4	33.6-38.9	24.5-28.9	31.0-35.7	22.8-26.9	26.1-32.2	20.2-24.4
Good	9:41-10:48 (min.)	12:30-14:30	10:46-12:00	13:31-15:54	11:01-12:30	14:31-16:30	11:31-13:00	15:56-17:30	12:31-14:30	16:31-19:00	14:00-16:15	17:31-19:30
O₂ Uptake ML/Kg/min.	45.2-50.9	35.0-38.9	42.5-46.4	33.0-36.9	41.0-44.9	31.5-35.6	39.0-43.7	29.0-32.8	35.8-40.9	27.0-31.4	32.2-36.4	24.5-30.2
Excellent	8:37-9:40 (min.)	11:50-12:29	9:45-10:45	12:30-13:30	10:00-11:00	13:00-14:30	10:30-11:30	13:45-15:55	11:00-12:30	14:30-16:30	11:15-13:59	16:30-17:30
O₂ Uptake ML/Kg/min.	51.0-55.9	39.0-41.9	46.5-52.4	37.0-40.9	45.0-49.4	35.7-40.0	43.8-48.0	32.9-36.9	41.0-45.3	31.5-35.7	36.5-44.2	30.3-31.4
Superior	<8:37 (min.)	<11:50	<9:45	<12:30	<10:00	<13:00	<10:30	<13:45	<11:00	<14:30	<11:15	<16:30
O₂ Uptake ML/Kg/min.	>56.0	>42.0	>52.5	>41.0	>49.5	>40.1	>48.1	>37.0	>45.4	>35.8	>44.3	>31.5

< means "less than"; > means "more than."
From The Aerobics Program for Total Well-being by Dr. Kenneth H. Cooper. Copyright © 1982 by Kenneth H. Cooper. Reprinted by permission of the publisher, M. Evans and Co., Inc., New York, NY 10017.

mains the same. With these principles in mind, let us analyze some basic programs to use to develop your CVR fitness.

Walking Program

The walking program is for beginners or for individuals who have been inactive for four weeks or longer. These individuals should start with a walking program to slowly develop the leg muscles, ligaments, and tendons to prevent painful stress injuries. Hastening development by running too early only delays training because of time lost due to injuries. Furthermore, if activity is too strenuous at the start, previous ligament or joint problems could be aggravated, further delaying development.

For older people and those with a low level of CVR condition, walking initially provides enough physical stress to increase CVR fitness. If you are in poor physical condition because of prior inactivity or obesity, heed the following suggestions:

Begin walking at a normal, easy, steady pace. Swing your arms rhythmically, take in a deep breath on every fifth breath

Table 4.3 Walking Program

Week	Walk (min.)	Frequency per week
1	15	4
2	15	5
3	18	5
4	20	5
5	23	5
6	25	5
7	28	5
8	30	5
9	33	5
10	35	5
11	40	5
12	45	5

By the end of the eighth week, you should be able to maintain a 15-minute mile pace.

and release the air as much as possible. Acquire good jogging shoes, making sure to land on your heel first at foot strike. After several weeks, or as you become accustomed to walking, increase your speed to the point of walking a mile in fifteen minutes or less. If you cannot maintain a brisk pace, periodically slow up for several seconds, then return to your more intense pace. After you have reached an intensity level of forty-five minutes (at a pace of fifteen minutes a mile), and providing you have no joint injuries, you can begin a walk-jog-walk program.

Walk-Jog-Walk Program

The walk-jog-walk technique of training represents the simplest approach for starting an exercise program to develop CVR fitness. This program has proven successful with school children, college students, medium-age adults, and even senior adults.

Jogging is defined by most exercise physiologists as running at a pace equivalent to an eight to twelve minute mile. A

Table 4.4 Walk-Jog-Walk Program

Week	Walk (min.)	Jog (min.)	Walk (min.)	Frequency per week
1	10	5	8	4
2	10	5	8	5
3	10	6	8	5
4	10	7	8	5
5	10	8	8	5
6	8	10	8	5
7	8	12	8	5
8	8	14	8	5
9	8	16	8	5
10	6	18	8	5
11	5	20	8	5
12	5	20	8	5

Check your pulse rate, making sure you reach your threshold heart rate of 70 percent.

brisk walk is defined as walking at a pace equivalent to a twelve-fifteen minute mile.

To begin your walk-jog-walk program, walk briskly for ten minutes. Then begin jogging at a pace comfortable to your level of fitness. (A comfortable pace is one in which you could carry on a short-sentence conversation as you jog without interruptions from rapid breathing.) Jog for five minutes; then cool down by walking at a slower pace for eight minutes. From table 4.4, notice the slow, gradual progression you should make.

Running Program

The running program is designed for individuals who want to progress further than the walk-jog-walk program or for well-conditioned individuals. The running program is designed for individuals who can run between a five- and eight-minute mile pace. So do not begin this program if you have been inactive for three weeks or longer. Progress slowly and enjoy your conditioning. Follow table 4.5 to determine your progress.

Table 4.5 Running Program

Week	Walk (min.)	Run (min.)	Walk (min.)	Frequency per week
1	3	20	5	5
2	3	20	5	5
3	3	22	5	5
4	3	22	5	5
5	3	25	5	5
6	3	25	5	5
7	3	28	5	5
8	3	28	5	5
9	3	32	5	5
10	3	35	5	5
11	3	40	5	5
12	3	40	5	5

Your running intensity should elevate your heart rate to the 70 percent level or higher.

Bicycling Program

To achieve a training effect with a bicycle, you must cycle slightly over twice as fast as you run to produce the same exercise heart rate. For bicycling to provide a heart rate stimulus of 70 percent of the difference between the maximum and resting rate. Also, warm up by cycling slowly for three minutes before attempting the specified time. Cool down by cycling slowly for three minutes at the conclusion of exercise. Table 4.6 presents a twelve-week bicycle program to develop CVR fitness.

Table 4.6 Bicycling Program

Week	Warm Up (min.)	Cycling Time (min.)	Cool Down (min.)	Frequency per week
1	3	15:00	3	5
2	3	15:00	3	5
3	3	18:00	3	5
4	3	20:00	3	5
5	3	23:00	3	5
6	3	25:00	3	5
7	3	28:00	3	5
8	3	30:00	3	5
9	3	33:00	3	5
10	3	35:00	3	5
11	3	38:00	3	5
12	3	40:00	3	5

Adjust the bicycle seat to the position in which your extended leg has only a slight bend at the knee joint.

Swimming Program

Many exercise physiologists and medical authorities advocate swimming as an ideal CVR conditioner. In comparison to jogging, there is less susceptibility to injury to the leg joints. Also the upper body muscles are worked harder for greater muscle development. Disadvantages are the accessibility of a pool and availability of an open lane that will enable you to swim unbothered.

Continuous swimming is most beneficial for improving CVR fitness. Develop your endurance to the point where you can swim the length of the pool nonstop for several minutes. You may want to use different strokes. Changing strokes systematically will strengthen all the muscles used for the different movements in the various strokes.

Check your pulse rate after a series of swims, making sure that it is at the 70 percent intensity level. Be sure to first warm up by walking back and forth across the shallow end of the pool for a minimum of three minutes. Cool down by walking in the same manner. For comparison, 100 yards of swimming equals approximately 400 yards of jogging. Therefore, jogging two miles is equivalent to about a half mile of swimming. A twelve-week swimming program is presented in table 4.7.

Table 4.7 Swimming Program

Week	Warm Up (min.)	Swimming Time (min.)	Cool Down (min.)	Frequency per week
1	3	8:00	3	5
2	3	8:00	3	5
3	3	10:00	3	5
4	3	12:00	3	5
5	3	15:00	3	5
6	3	18:00	3	5
7	3	20:00	3	5
8	3	23:00	3	5
9	3	25:00	3	5
10	3	25:00	3	5
11	3	28:00	3	5
12	3	30:00	3	5

Wear swim goggles to protect your eyes from chemical irritants in the pool water.

Stationary Cycling Program

For those unable to walk, jog, or swim because of orthopedic problems, the stationary exercise bike provides a good stimulus for the CVR system. The exercise bike has adjustable pedal resistance which, if properly adjusted to your level of fitness, can elevate your exercise heart rate to the recommended 70 percent level. The bicycle seat should be high enough so that the extended leg in the down position is almost straight. Warm up by cycling for three minutes at zero resistance, and cool down at the conclusion of the exercise in the same way. Table 4.8 presents a twelve-week stationary cycling program.

Table 4.8 Stationary Bicycling Program

Week	Warm Up (min.) zero resistance	Cycling Time (min.)	Cool Down (min.) zero resistance	Frequency per week
1	3	8:00	3	5
2	3	8:00	3	5
3	3	10:00	3	5
4	3	13:00	3	5
5	3	15:00	3	5
6	3	18:00	3	5
7	3	20:00	3	5
8	3	23:00	3	5
9	3	25:00	3	5
10	3	25:00	3	5
11	3	28:00	3	5
12	3	30:00	3	5

Some individuals pedal while watching their favorite television program.

These programs which were presented are only a few of the modes in which you can develop CVR fitness. Other programs for developing CVR fitness are given in books by Kenneth Cooper[1] and Getchell.[2] If you follow one of these programs to its conclusion, you will notice a difference in the way you feel and look. Your body's physiology will improve which also brings an improvement in your psychological outlook, which improves your happiness.

Guidelines for CVR Training

Probably the worst thing that you can do to begin your CVR program is grab your old tennis shoes, head for the nearest track, and run at top speed around the track. That could cause more harm than good. You must prepare yourself physically before you rush into cardiovascular exercise, or someone may have to rush you to the hospital. Please follow these guidelines and protect yourself from harm and injury.

1. *Get a medical examination,* especially if you are over thirty-five years of age. The medical examination should consist of a standard and stress electrocardiogram (ECG); resting and exercise blood pressure measurements; fasting blood sugar (glucose), cholesterol, triglyceride, and high-density lipoprotein determinations; and evaluation of any orthopedic problem.

2. *Warm up before exercising.* Before beginning a CVR training program, subject your total body to a proper warm up. The warm up is a precaution against unnecessary injuries and muscle soreness. It stimulates the heart and lungs moderately and progressively, as well as increases the blood flow and the blood and muscle temperatures gradually. It also prepares you mentally for the approaching strenuous workout.

The following five-minute warm-up routine is recommended. During the first two minutes, do stretching exercises for arms, legs, and back (figs. 4.5—4.7). During the third and fourth minutes, do sit-ups, push-ups, and back raisers (figs. 4.8—4.10). During the final minute, walk or jog very slowly. Strive to walk or jog flat-footed as much as possible during the warm up. This gives the tendons and ligaments in the feet and ankles a chance to stretch gradually, helping to avoid possible irritation from sudden stress.

The time required for warm up varies with each individual. Sweat indicates that the core temperature has increased and more intense conditioning can be done. Keep in mind that cold weather requires longer warm-up times.

3. *Cool down after exercising.* Cool down is a tapering-off period after completion of the main workout and is as important to the body as the warm up. During the CVR exercise, the large muscles of the legs provide a boost to the circulating blood and help return it to the heart and lungs where the ex-

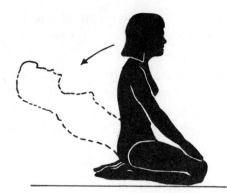

Fig. 4.5 Stretching anterior thigh muscles (quadriceps). Sit for one minute.

Fig. 4.6 Stretching posterior thigh muscles (hamstrings). Stretch for eight seconds. Repeat five times.

Fig. 4.7 Calf muscles stretching. Move buttocks toward wall. Keep heels on floor.

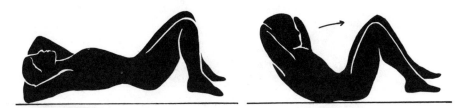

Fig. 4.8 Sit-up. Keep knees bent; tuck chin in; elbows forward; lift chest to knees; return to floor slowly.

Fig. 4.9a Push-up (men). Keep back straight; touch chest to floor.

Fig. 4.9b Modified push-up (women).

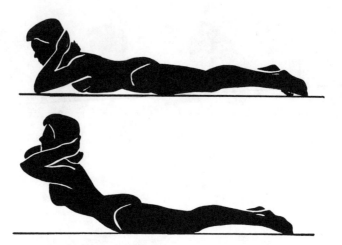

Fig. 4.10a   Trunk raiser. Keep legs on floor; raise trunk as high as possible.

Fig. 4.10b   Leg raiser. Raise legs as high as possible.

change of oxygen and carbon dioxide takes place. As the muscle relaxes after exertion, blood fills the veins. It is not allowed to flow backward because of the valves in the veins. During exercise the squeezing action of the leg muscles provide about half of the pumping action, while the heart provides the other half. Walking or slow jogging, as in the cool down, allows the muscle pump to continue to work until the total volume of blood being pumped is decreased to where the heart can handle it without help from the muscles.

Always reduce your exercise pace very slowly, never abruptly. Do not stop instantly or sit down after you finish vigorous exercise or the blood will pool in your legs and you can faint from lack of blood to the brain.

4. *Exercise within your tolerance.* Do not push yourself to the extent of becoming overly tired. This is not only dangerous to your health, but defeats the purpose of exercise. If your body does not feel strong when you first awake, then you may be overtraining.

5. *Progress slowly.* In exercise, hurrying your fitness development does not work; it merely invites trouble, such as muscle and joint injuries. You do not have to be first in everything you do. Take your time in your development of fitness. Gradually work up to your exercise goals.

6. *Get adequate rest and nutrition.* Your body may suffer from chronic fatigue if nutrition and rest are inadequate. No matter how hard or long you train the CVR system, optimal results will not be achieved if nutrition and rest are poor.

7. *Exercise regularly.* Consistency and regularity are necessary for strengthening the CVR system. Spasmodic exercise can be dangerous. Your body is similar to a busy warehouse which is constantly moving goods in and out. Your exercise benefits cannot be stored; you need to add benefits daily. For every one week you cease to exercise, it takes nearly two weeks to regain the previous fitness level. Just as food intake is used up almost daily, so are the benefits of exercise unless they are replenished with more exercise.

8. *Wear proper shoes.* A faulty pair of exercise shoes can erase your good intentions to exercise as well as cause foot, leg, or hip injuries. Good shoes can eliminate many of the hazards associated with walking or jogging, such as blisters and stress to the feet, legs, and hips. Canvas tennis shoes are not good for walking and jogging, because they are too heavy and usually give poor foot support to the ligaments and bones. The training type of shoe used by most long-distant runners is recommended for jogging. These have a leather or nylon upper; a good, cushioned, multilayered, spongelike sole; and a strong heel counter. Quality is the key here. Exercise participants should buy the best shoe they can afford. Anyone unsure about what shoes to purchase would be wise to consult with someone who does a lot of long-distance running.

9. *Exercise cautiously in hot weather.* Never exercise vigorously when a combined temperature and humidity reach 165 or above (that is, 85° F. and 80 percent humidity). Exercising over this recommended rate increases susceptibility to heat stroke. Never allow your body temperature to elevate above 105° F. The best method of cooling your body during exercise is through evaporation. If humidity is above 80 percent, the evaporative processes of the body do not function properly, because the humid atmosphere cannot accept any more moisture that would come from the body. The body temperature will quickly rise above the danger level. If you live in a hot, and humid climate, you may have to exercise early in the morning or late at night. Wear clothes that allow your body to cool itself by evaporation. Never wear a sweat suit or rubberized suit that promotes sweating. Do not try to lose weight by sweating it off. This is not only dangerous, but you will gain the weight back when you drink fluids.

10. *Dress appropriately in cold conditions.* Most people overdress when they exercise in cold temperatures. Dress to feel comfortably warm during the exercise period without profuse sweating. Usually, one or two layers of light clothing, a knit cap covering the head and ears, and knit gloves are sufficient. In very cold weather, a ski mask can be worn to protect the face and warm the air as it goes into the lungs. Always run with the wind in the latter stage of your exercise. The chill factor is increased when you run into the wind. If you run against the wind after sweating has increased, the chilling effects of the wind will be magnified.

Regular systemic CVR exercise is an important key to a happy life, as it promotes physical, mental, psychological, and social fitness. It provides an outlet for emotional tensions and promotes self-confidence, wholesome social activity, and good sportsmanship. It enhances the sense of general well-being that provides the willpower to confront and master the difficult personal challenges faced each day. But remember to heed these safety precautions: start slowly, progress slowly, and do not overdo.

CHAPTER 5

Happiness Involves Reducing Body Composition

Whose end is destruction, whose God is their belly (Phil. 3:19).

In the good old days, before progress lured us off the farm and made us affluent and fat, we had strong muscles and simple diets. When the cow was in the barn and the manure on the fields, the meat was pure and the vegetables organic. Before the advent of giant agribusiness, wheat was rich enough to make bread the staff of life. The protein content of bread was 18 to 20 percent in 1886, whereas it was 9 to 12 percent in 1982. We were poor in things, and food distribution, processing, and preserving were not all they could be. But the 45 percent of the American population who lived and ate on the farms were well furnished with natural vitamins and minerals.

Affluence turned our diet rich and our bodies soft. By the 1980s the average American was consuming 130 pounds of fat, 250 pounds of meat and poultry, 140 pounds of refined and processed sugars, and 485 twelve-ounce bottles or cans of soda per year. The Standard American Diet (SAD) has become increasingly dominated by highly refined carbohydrates and fast foods. Only 20 percent of our calories (compared to 40 percent in 1900) comes from fresh fruit, vegetables, and whole grains. Because most of our food is raised with the aid of chemical fertilizers and pesticides, we ingest an unknown quantity of poisons such as the infamous Agent Orange used to defoliate Vietnam, in addition to a smorgasbord of perhaps as many as 1,800 chemicals (which averages out to five pounds in a year's time) that are routinely added to processed food to color, preserve, and flavor. Unfortunately, it seems true "you can't sell nutrition." "All people want is Coke and potato chips" are the

Fig. 5.1 Physically active people have more fun.

words of biochemist Arthur Odell, former director of special projects, General Mills research division.

Diet and Disease

Epidemiological studies that compare diet and disease profiles of different groups of people have amassed a growing body of evidence that SAD (which is being adopted increasingly by affluent people everywhere) is associated with high rates of heart disease, hypertension, diabetes, and cancer of the breast, stomach, and colon—the very diseases that are at epidemic level in the United States. Let us examine the role of diet as it relates to these diseases.

Heart Disease

The role of cholesterol, saturated fats, and triglycerides as it relates to heart disease has been examined in chapter 4. Let us turn our attention to other diet-related causes that research has linked to heart disease.

It is obvious that Americans are consuming too much cholesterol, saturated fats, and triglycerides in their diet (primarily from animal fat). But, it simply doesn't make sense that a staple of human consumption for eons, animal fat, should turn out to be the cause of a sudden increase in heart attacks in less than a century. The course is not a simple one, for there is a complexity of biochemical and nutritional factors that are involved in maintaining health and in preventing such disasters as heart attacks. Multiple factors are the rule in any medical question. Let us examine three of these factors that research has linked to heart disease. It must be noted that these factors are not conclusive in determining heart disease in every individual, but a high relationship has been established among these three factors and heart disease.

Three major changes in the environment—about thirty years apart from each other—suggest why this century ushered in heart attacks. These changes were essentially dietary: (1) the introduction of refined and bleached flour; (2) large-scale chlorination of water supplies: and (3) homogenization of milk. All three contributed; no single factor is the villain, for all three affect each human differently.

In the technological advance of milling flour, the wheat germ is systematically stripped from the grain, along with the B vitamins, vitamin E, and such trace substances as magnesium, manganese, and chromium. It took nearly a century for researchers to determine that nutrient-deficiency diseases such as pellagra, beriberi, anemia, and a variety of other syndromes resulted from a lack of multiple B vitamins which might be due to milling flour. In 1941 a federal agency mandated the enrichment of white flour with B_1, B_2, B_3, and the mineral iron. The authorities put three vitamins and one mineral into white flour, but left out twenty vitamins and minerals. At that time medical authorities simply didn't know about the vital roles of vitamins E, B_6, folic acid, and a whole range of trace minerals and how they contributed to our health.

Even today, knowing what we do now, the millers are still enriching our flour with: thiamine (vitamin B_1), riboflavin (vitamin B_2), niacin (vitamin B_3), and iron. The millers are still leaving out very essential vitamins such as E, and B_6. Vitamin

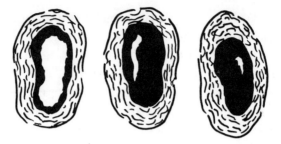

Fig. 5.2 Process of atherosclerosis. Notice the buildup of fats in the artery.

E helps neutralize free radicals (which are electrically charged molecules that cause damage to the cells in the blood vessels [intima]). These free radicals are now believed by most researchers to be the most important cause of atherosclerosis. Vitamin E is also known to protect against unwanted blood clotting. Vitamin B_6 has been found to protect against the toxic effects of the amino acid *homocysteine,* a known cause of atherosclerosis. We would be wise to consume whole-grain products instead of refined-grain products.

Thirty years after we had become accustomed to white bread on the table, along came a second precursor of heart disease. In 1910 our water supplies began to be treated with chlorine, a chemical that kills germs even in water standing in pipes. This public health measure was widely adopted throughout the country; today there are over 40,000 municipal water districts in the United States and all their supplies are chlorinated. Again, it wasn't known then, and is scarcely mentioned now, that even in the minute quantities sufficient to kill germs, chlorine can undermine the body's defenses against atherosclerosis. Chlorine creates electrically charged molecules called free radicals, which can combine with alpha tocopherol (vitamin E) and eliminate this vitamin from your system. In addition, free radicals can directly damage the intima of blood vessels and so create the environment for the formation of plaques. It is now being recognized that chlorine is dangerous enough to be considered a pollutant. Chlorine also has been found to interact with industrial wastes in waters to produce carcinogens (cancer-causing chemicals).

We can avoid white flour, but what about chlorinated water? We can let our drinking water stand in an open container at room temperature for half a day and the chlorine will evaporate. We could boil our water; or we could invest in a home-distillation system. In our so-called modern society, all of this may seem ludicrous, but until a logical successor to chlorine is found (ozone treatment works at the water plant, but not in the pipes), our drinking water will continue to be a contributing factor to heart disease.

Finally, some thirty years after the widespread chlorination of our water supply began, a third dietary change occurred in this country that would further weaken our protection against artherosclerosis, the homogenization of milk. The homogenized fat droplets bypass the liver and are absorbed directly into the lymphatic system and then into the bloodstream.

There is an enzyme in cow's milk, xanthine oxidase, which is known to irritate the lining of blood vessels. If this xanthine oxidase enzyme were not carried by the homogenized fat droplets in milk, it would be eliminated by chemical action in the body's protector, the liver.

Thus, we are faced with the dilemma of drinking homogenized whole milk, with its wide variety of nutrients, and thereby also ingesting xanthine oxidase in a dangerous form. There are some alternatives to this dilemma. We can drink low-fat milk. Or we can heat our milk to 92° C for five seconds to inactivate the enzyme.

In any discussion of complex dietary health issues, we must remind ourselves not to run to extreme positions. But there are some simple precautions that we can take to help us avoid heart disease.

(1) Eat whole-grain flour products instead of refined flour products.
(2) Filter or eliminate chlorine from your drinking water.
(3) Drink low-fat milk.

(4) Maintain a normal weight. Of all the treatments that have been able to lower serum cholesterol and improve atherosclerosis, again weight reduction stands out.

(5) Exercise the cardiovascular system at least thirty minutes a day, three to six days a week.

Diabetes

In 1982, diabetes mellitus was the sixth most prominent cause of death from disease in the United States. Diabetes mellitus affects approximately eleven million individuals in America, 1.6 million of whom are children from ages one to eighteen. Diabetes is increasing by nearly 7 percent annually. At this alarming rate, an American today, with a life span of seventy-four years, has more than a one-in-five chance of developing this disorder. Diabetics frequently experience greatly accelerated degeneration of blood vessels, which leads to blindness, kidney disease, heart attack, stroke, gangrene in the extremities, and nervous system problems.

Simply put, diabetes occurs when the glucose level (blood sugar) in the body reaches an abnormally high level (approximately 140 mg). Glucose is a carbohydrate that contains carbon, hydrogen, and oxygen molecules. Carbohydrates are found in our food sources such as starches and sugars. Most glucose formed from dietary sugars and starches is stored in the liver where it is stockpiled as the molecule, glycogen. Muscles normally use glucose from the bloodstream for energy. If the body needs more glucose than is available in the bloodstream, it taps the liver's glycogen stores, reconverting the glycogen to sugar for energy.

Insulin is the major control agent for maintaining a normal blood glucose level. Insulin is produced in the pancreas by beta cells. Insulin facilitates the use of blood sugar and prevents its rise to abnormal levels. Sometimes the blood sugar decreases to an unsafe lower limit (below 70 mg). When this occurs, another hormone secreted by the alpha cells in the pancreas called glucagon comes to the rescue. It has the opposite action to insulin. It helps break down liver glycogen, raising blood glucose levels to normal as needed. It acts as a counterbalance to excess insulin and as such is often used to treat insulin shock.

In diabetes, production of insulin is either lacking, insufficient, or cannot be utilized properly by the body. Without the necessary amount of, or ability to utilize, insulin, the body cannot use glucose for energy, or store it as glycogen, which results in glucose accumulation in the blood. When the glucose level is too high the resulting condition is hyperglycemia. When too low, the condition is hypoglycemia. Extreme hyperglycemia results in a diabetic coma.

There are several causes of diabetes. Hereditary factors play an important role in diabetes. People with diabetic parents or close relatives, therefore, may often be predisposed to diabetes. In fact, if both parents are diabetic, the probability for a child to develop the disease increases 100 percent. Therefore, blood relatives of known diabetics should be tested periodically to determine whether the disease is present.

Obesity is also a predisposing factor in diabetes, especially in adults. Eighty-five percent of adults with diabetic onset at maturity are overweight or have been overweight prior to the disease. Persons over forty-five years of age appear to be more vulnerable. In fact, one American over forty-five acquires diabetes every minute. Research has determined that obesity is an accelerating factor in maturity-onset diabetes. Individuals with diabetic tendencies may get the disease earlier if they become overweight.

Diabetes may also be caused by nutritional factors that damage the pancreas, impair glucose tolerance, or interfere with the function of the beta cells. Researchers speculate that high intakes of sugar and refined carbohydrate products, complex carbohydrate consumption, and consumption of dietary fiber are responsible.

In my opinion, consuming too much refined sugar is one of the major culprits in causing diabetes. Consuming too much sugar raises the glucose level which overworks the pancreas.

In 1982 Americans consumed an average of 140 pounds of refined sugar, which would be an equivalent of consuming thirty-six teaspoons of sugar a day. Most Americans deny that they consume such an incredible amount of refined sugar, but most soft drinks contain ten to twelve teaspoons of refined sugar in a twelve-ounce container. Someone is drinking a lot of soft drinks, for soft-drink companies revealed that in 1982 for every American in the US they consumed 485 soft drinks, which did not include fountain drinks. Drinking more than one soft drink a day and eating other sugar-filled foods lends credence to these statistics. One survey revealed that 92 percent of all items sold in a supermarket contained sugar. (See table 5.1.) We've become a nation of sugarholics. Eating thirty-six teaspoons of sugar a day places an extra burden on our insulin production. No wonder after forty-five years of this abuse the pancreas ceases to function properly and maturity-onset diabetes occurs.

Research suggests that fiber-depleted diets have also contributed to diabetes. Diabetes was rare in primitive populations which consume diets high in less refined carbohydrate foods. Recent research suggests that consumption of dietary fiber influences blood insulin and glucose levels. In diabetes,

Fig. 5.3 A typical selection of junk food served at a church fellowship.

Table 5.1
Refined Sugar in Beverages and Food

Item	Portion	Teaspoonsfuls of Granulated Sugar
Beverages		
Cola drinks	12 oz.	10
Ginger ale	12 oz.	12
Highball	6 oz.	2½
Root beer	12 oz.	8
Seven-up	12 oz.	10½
Sweet cider	1 cup	6
Dairy Products		
Ice cream cone	1	3½
Ice cream soda	1	5
Ice cream sundae	1	7
Malted milkshake	10 oz.	5½
Desserts		
Custard	½ cup	2
Fruit gelatin	½ cup	4½
Apple pie	1 slice	7
Cherry pie	1 slice	10
Cream pie	1 slice	4
Lemon pie	1 slice	7
Banana pudding	½ cup	2
Chocolate pudding	½ cup	4
Sherbet	½ cup	9
Cakes and Cookies		
Angel food cake	4 oz. piece	7
Cheesecake	4 oz. piece	2
Chocolate cake (iced)	4 oz. piece	10
Coffee cake	4 oz. piece	4½
Cupcake	1	6
Strawberry shortcake	1 serving	4
Brownie	1 (¾ oz.)	3
Chocolate eclair	1	7
Doughnut (glazed)	1	6
Oatmeal cookie	1	2

Candies		
Chocolate milk bar	1 (⅕ oz.)	2½
Chewing gum	1 stick	½
Chocolate mints	1	2
Fudge	1 oz. square	4½
Jelly beans	1	2
Peanut brittle	1 oz.	3½
Canned Fruits and Juices		
Canned fruit juices	½ cup	2
Canned peaches	2 halves	3½
Fruit salad	½ cup	3½
Jams and Jellies		
Apple butter	1 tablespoon	1
Jelly	1 tablespoon	4-6
Strawberry jam	1 tablespoon	4

Information supplied by Gly-oxide, distributed by Marion Laboratories, Inc., 10236 Bunker Ridge Road, Kansas City, MO.

increases in serum glucose are lower after consuming a fiber-containing meal.

Research cannot prove conclusively that diabetes is caused by these nutritional shortcomings, but most medical authorities agree that Americans need to reduce their consumption of refined sugar and refined carbohydrates and eat more fiber-containing foods.

Cancer of Colon

The United States has the highest rate of colon cancer in the world. About forty-five of every 100,000 American men between the ages of thirty-five and sixty-four develop cancer of the colon and rectum. According to the American Cancer Society, cancer of the colon and rectum is now the first and most common form of lethal cancer. Nearly 100,000 new cases of colon and rectum cancer occur each year, resulting in almost 50,000 deaths. This means that every five minutes someone develops this form of cancer and every ten minutes someone dies from it. These shocking figures make it even more urgent for Americans to promptly restore essential foods to their daily diets.

Comparison studies were made between African nations and numerous industrialized countries concerning diet as a cause of degenerative diseases. Researchers noticed that African nations had a low percentage of heart attacks, cancer of the colon and rectum, diverticulosis (pouching out of the large intestinal wall), appendicitis, hemorrhoids, varicose veins, and phlebitis (blood clots in the leg veins). Investigation revealed the following differences: (1) Africans had more massive, heavier less odoriferous bowel movements than Americans; (2) Africans moved their food through the body three times faster than Americans; (3) Africans ate about three times as much roughage or vegetable fiber as Americans.

These findings have a significant relationship to our health, especially for cancer of the colon and rectum. Let's examine what research now tells us about the effects of fiber on God's temple.

Fiber holds water and, in doing so, provides bulk. In its journey through the gastrointestinal tract, food is bathed in digestive juices and bile. These, added to the natural fluid content of food, make the mixture (called chyme) semifluid and gruel-like. Nutrients, of course, are absorbed in the small intestine. The remaining wet material then arrives in the colon, and here a significant portion of the fluid is sopped up and returned to the bloodstream for reuse. In an average day, some twelve ounces of chyme can enter the colon, but only four ounces can pass out as stool, thanks to fluid reabsorption.

If sufficient fiber is present, it can hold on to enough fluid to make for a soft, voluminous stool. Otherwise, there may be a series of abnormal consequences.

Constipation.—Without the fluid-retaining activity of fiber, stools tend to be small in volume and hard, pebbly, and slow moving. The stools of native Africans have been found to weigh as much as 500 grams a day compared with the 100-gram average in the constipated American. And the transit time (the interval between when a meal is eaten and when the

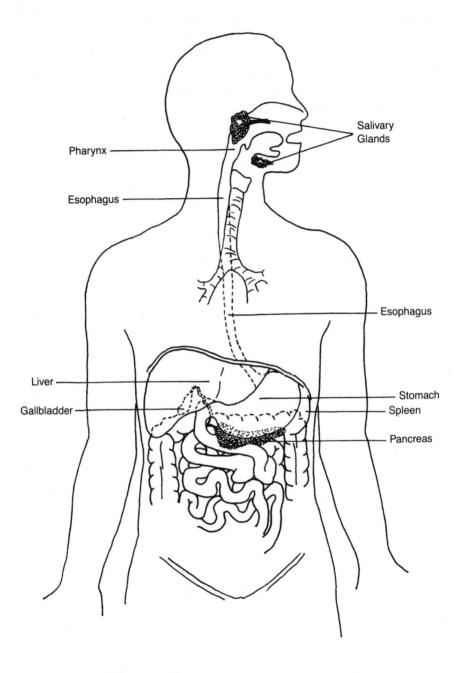

Fig. 5.4 The Digestive System

remains are eliminated) averages only thirty-five hours for Africans and up to ninety hours for Americans. Study after study has shown that nearly all patients with constipation are helped by a liberal intake of fiber-rich foods.

Diverticular disease.—A diverticulum is a small bag or sac protruding from the intestinal wall. There may be hundreds of diverticula in the colon. These pouches can trap feces, and about 32 percent of people with diverticula develop inflammation (diverticulitis) that can produce severe pain in the lower left abdomen, along with nausea, vomiting, distension, chills, and fever. Medical treatment sometimes helps, but surgery often is required.

Today, high-fiber diets are used in the treatment of diverticular disease and as a means of avoiding the condition. Several physicians report that an increase in fiber intake has helped avoid the need for surgery.

Colon cancer.—This malignancy is believed to be the result of cancer-inducing products from bacteria in the bowel. Both excess fat and inadequate fiber intake have been linked in producing this carcinogenic bacteria. Excess fat intake can increase the flow of bile acids, on which these bacteria act to produce carcinogenic products.

Adequate fiber intake helps in several ways. Whatever carcinogens are produced will be diluted in the large stools associated with a fiber-rich diet. And with the faster transit time, there is less time for carcinogens to act on the bowel wall before elimination.

Fiber sources.—One excellent way to add fiber to your diet is to eat more vegetables and fruits, for fiber is found in plant cell walls. There is naturally no dietary fiber in meat, fish, fats, milk, or sugar. (See table 5.2.)

Seeds such as whole sesame and sunflower, along with such seed-filled berries as raspberries, blackberries, and strawberries, are rich in fiber. So are some, but not all, breakfast cereals. You can pick from a number of high-fiber cereals: old-fashioned, slow-cooking (not instant) oatmeal; whole-grain wheat cereals designed to be cooked, shredded wheat, cereals

Table 5.2
Table of Dietary Fiber

Food	Portion Size	Grams of Fiber
High-fiber and bran cereals	½ Cup	up to 13.5*
Baked Beans	½ Cup	8.3
Apple	1 Medium	7.9
Broccoli, cooked	1 Medium stalk	7.4
Coconut, shredded	1 Piece (2″ × 2″ × ½″)	6.1
Spinach, cooked	½ Cup	5.7
Blackberries	½ Cup	5.3
Almonds	¼ Cup	5.1
Kidney beans	½ Cup	4.5
Cabbage, shredded, boiled	½ Cup	4.3
Peas, cooked	½ Cup	4.2
White beans	½ Cup	4.2
Banana	1 Medium	4.0
Corn	½ Cup	3.9
Potato	1 Medium	3.9
Pear	1 Medium	3.8
Lima beans, cooked	½ Cup	3.5
Sweet potato	1 Medium	3.5
Pinto beans	½ Cup	3.1
Peanuts, chopped	¼ Cup	2.9
Brown rice, raw	¼ Cup	2.8
Cornflakes	1 Cup	2.8
Orange	1 Medium	2.6
Raisins	¼ Cup	2.8
Brussels sprouts	4	2.4
Peanut butter	2 Tablespoons	2.4
Whole wheat bread	1 Slice	2.4
Carrots, raw	1 Medium	2.3
Beets	½ Cup	2.1
Peaches	1 Medium	2.1
Zucchini, raw	½ Cup	2.0
String beans	½ Cup	1.9
Tomato, raw	1 Medium	1.8
Miller's bran	1 Tablespoon	1.6
Onions, cooked	½ Cup	1.6

Strawberries	½ Cup	1.6
Walnuts, chopped	¼ Cup	1.6
Asparagus, chopped	½ Cup	1.2
Cherries	10	1.1
Pineapple	1 Piece (3½" × ¾")	1.0
Cauliflower, raw	½ Cup	1.0
White bread	1 Slice	.8
Celery, raw	1 Stalk	.7
Plums	3 Medium	.6
Cucumbers, sliced	½ Cup	.2

*Cereals vary in fiber content. Check individual products for specific information. Information supplied by: Southgate, D.A.T. 1978. Dietary Fiber: Analysis and food sources. *Amer. J. Clin. Nutr.* 31: 5107.

labeled as being all bran or made up of a high percentage of bran.

An important substitution is bread made from whole-wheat or whole-rye flour in place of white bread. Whole-meal flour can be used at home for biscuits, waffles, pancakes, etc. Use brown unpolished rich when possible. And use whole-meal spaghetti and macaroni in place of the routine kind. Also, you can add unprocessed bran (a couple of teaspoons at a time to suit your taste) to cereals, soups or whole-meal flour.

Personally, I feel we should consume between fifteen to twenty-five grams of fiber each day to help us afford a better protection against these digestive disorders. The best way to judge whether you are getting enough fiber in your diet is to check your stools, which should become softer and well-formed, and be passed without straining.

Hypertension

Hypertension is the most prevalent heart and blood vessel disease, afflicting an estimated 18 percent of adults in the industrialized world. It is also perhaps the most dangerous, usually striking without symptoms and often abetting other cardiovascular killers. One of these cardiovascular killers is a stroke, which is usually caused by the blood pounding the brain's arterial walls with extra force causing them to roughen and wear out. Paralysis or death usually occurs when the brain's blood is impeded in any way.

When the heart contracts, the blood pressure rises to its highest level, which is called systolic pressure. When the heart relaxes, the pressure drops to its minimum, called the diastolic pressure. This degree of variance is high and low pressure causing the blood to circulate throughout the body. Any abnormality in this pressure distinguishes the ill from the healthy.

There are three main causes of blood pressure abnormalities: physical, chemical, and electrical. Physical regulators are the arteries, which become hardened (arterosclerosis) and narrowed with fatty deposits (atherosclerosis) thus increasing resistance to blood flow and boosting pressure. Affecting the chemical regulators may be tumors of the adrenal glands, which may cause the glands to secrete abnormal amounts of hormones, thus elevating pressure. A diseased kidney may also release more renin than usual, which causes a corresponding rise in pressure. Finally, when the nerve (electrical) regulators fail, they erroneously indicate that pressure is normal when it actually is high. These specific causes of hypertension are readily identifiable but occur so rarely that they are considered secondary causes. Most doctors cannot tell which regulator is malfunctioning, or why. Such blood pressure is labeled essential or idiopathic, which indicates undetermined origin.

Medical authorities categorize blood pressure levels differently. What one considers normal, another may view as elevated. A strong medical consensus suggests that blood pressure of 120/80 is normal and desirable for a healthy adult. A reading of 140/90 generally is regarded as the threshold of hypertension, and the patient is often placed under medical care. Most doctors classify any reading higher than 160/95 as dangerously hypertensive. At the other end of the scale, a value of 90/50 is considered as hypotensive (low blood pressure) and may indicate illness. Research done on Olympic

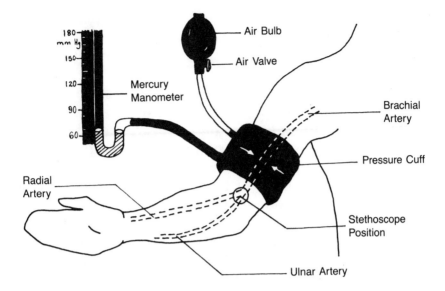

Fig. 5.5 Apparatus for measuring blood pressure

track performers reveal blood pressure readings of 110/50. Notice the low diastolic pressure which indicates an open artery free from fatty buildup.

According to insurance companies' actuarial data, longevity is also affected significantly by blood pressure. A thirty-five-year-old man with a blood pressure of 120/80 can expect to live an additional forty-one and one half years, but a man of the same age with a blood pressure of 140/95 can expect to live only thirty-seven and one half years more. A thirty-five-year-old man with a blood pressure of 150/100 has a life expectancy of only twenty-five years. Raise the numbers slightly and the risk rises significantly.

Doctors today know how to reduce blood pressure to non-threatening levels in about 85 percent of the cases. Sometimes the treatment is remarkably simple.

    (1) *Don't be overweight.*—Obesity imposes an added burden on the heart because blood volume increases with body weight. Approximately 200 miles of new capillaries are required to supply every additional pound of fat tissue. And to circulate the extra blood through the

larger body, the heart must pump at higher pressure.

(2) *Don't smoke.*—The nicotine in tabacco smoke is believed to constrict blood vessels and raise blood pressure.

(3) *Don't drink alcohol.*—Alcohol constricts the coronary arteries that supply the heart muscle with blood. This places an extra burden on the heart and pressure.

(4) *Reduce sodium and salt intake.*—The sodium in salt makes the body retain fluid. Increased fluid retention raises the volume of blood flowing through the circulatory system and raises the blood pressure. A diet that restricts sodium intake leads to lowering blood pressure in nearly 50 percent of the cases. This means eliminating or sharply curbing consumption of salty foods such as dill pickles, luncheon meats, corned beef, bacon, ham, canned soups, and many commercially canned or frozen vegetables. Seasonings such as catsup, relishes, soy sauce, and table salt should be avoided altogether.

(5) *Start an exercise program.*—Research indicates that a regular exercise program reduces certain forms of hypertension by reducing neuromuscular tension. Reducing tension enables relaxation, which lowers blood pressure. Many doctors advocate specific relaxation techniques to treat high blood pressure. Some methods include yoga, meditation, and biofeedback techniques which help borderline hypertensions reach normal blood pressure levels.

If blood pressure cannot be lowered by changing your lifestyle, then suitable drug therapy, prescribed by a physician, is mandatory. *Never* stop taking your antihypertensive medication without first consulting your physician.

Am I Fat?

After reading how diet and obesity affects health, the next question that should be answered is, "How fat am I?" Possibly the simplest test for fatness is to stand naked in front of a mirror and closely examine your body. If you look fat, then you are fat. Another simple way is to compare your height and weight to norms set up by insurance companies (see table 5.4). These charts are not always reliable, however, for these tables have been devised on desirable weights, not actual weights. These desirable weights are derived from people showing the lowest mortality rates, and such individuals happen to be below the average weight. Another weakness in these charts can be shown by the example of the fat-determination studies done on the Dallas Cowboy football team. Running back Tony Dorsett was determined to have 4 percent body fat, which is classified as excellent; yet the height-weight tables revealed that he was twenty pounds overweight. Strong individuals with much muscle development can appear fatter than they actually are. Also, fat people will look at these charts and automatically determine that they have large frames, when they actually could

Fig. 5.6 Some people can eat anything and not get fat.

Table 5.3
Determination of Relative Frame Size of the Human Body
Wrist Circumference

Sex	Small Frame Inches	Medium Frame Inches	Large Frame Inches
Male	6½″ or less	6½″-7½″	7½″ or more
Female	5½″ or less	5½″-6″	6″ or more

Table 5.4
Ideal Weight for Men and Women—According to Height and Frame, Age 25 and Over (weight in pounds, in indoor clothing)

**Height with shoes on
(Men—1 inch heels;
Women—1 inch heels)**

Feet-Inches		Small Frame	Medium Frame	Large Frame
		Men		
5	2	128-134	131-141	138-150
5	3	130-136	133-143	140-153
5	4	132-138	135-145	142-156
5	5	134-140	137-148	144-160
5	6	136-142	139-151	146-164
5	7	138-145	142-154	149-168
5	8	140-148	145-157	152-172
5	9	142-151	148-160	155-176
5	10	144-154	151-163	158-180
5	11	146-157	154-166	161-184
6	0	149-160	157-170	164-188
6	1	152-164	160-174	168-192
6	2	155-168	164-178	172-197
6	3	158-172	167-182	176-202
6	4	162-176	171-187	181-207

Feet-Inches		Small Frame	Medium Frame	Large Frame
		Women		
4	10	102-111	109-121	118-131
4	11	103-113	111-123	120-134
5	0	104-115	113-126	122-137
5	1	106-118	115-129	125-140
5	2	108-121	118-132	128-143
5	3	111-124	121-135	131-147
5	4	114-127	124-138	134-151
5	5	117-130	127-141	137-155
5	6	120-133	130-144	140-159
5	7	123-136	133-147	143-163
5	8	126-139	136-150	146-167
5	9	129-142	139-153	149-170
5	10	132-145	142-156	152-173
5	11	135-148	145-159	155-176
6	0	138-151	148-162	158-179

Courtesy of Metropolitan Insurance Company, Health and Safety Education Division.

have small frames. Tables 5.3 and 5.4 can help you determine your frame size and true weight.

Frame size is determined from wrist circumference, which should be measured with a tape measure at the smallest point above the two bones which protrude on each side. Pull the tape measure as tight as possible.

Another method of estimating fatness is by measuring the thickness of fatfold with a skinfold caliper. Because much of the body fat is just under the skin and overlaying muscles, the thickness of a pinch of skin and fat can be used as an indicator of total body fatness. Most physical education departments at colleges and church recreation ministers are skilled in determining percentage of body fatness with skinfold measurements. Contact one of these professionals in your area and determine how fat you really are.

Overweight for men is usually considered between 15 to 20 percent body fatness. Obesity for men is body fatness that is greater than 20 percent. Being overweight for women is considered between 25-30 percent body fatness, whereas, obesity is considered to be greater than 30 percent body fatness. We should strive to keep our total percentage of body fat below 15 percent for men and 20 percent for women. We need to lose that excess body fat that causes spiritual, physical, mental, and emotional havoc to God's temple. Probably the most practical criterion for evaluating fatness is the length of our belt. Remember the longer the belt, the shorter the life.

How Can I Lose Weight?

After it has been determined that you are overweight, the next question is obvious. How can I lose this excess weight? Did you ever wonder why some skinny people can eat anything they desire without gaining a pound while others seem to gain a pound by just smelling a piece of cake? There are several factors that greatly modify an individual's intake and need for calories, and it is important that we recognize these if a proper understanding and control of body weight is to be gained.

The first factor to be considered is basal metabolic rate (BMR). The BMR referes to the rate at which the body uses calories to maintain itself during a state of complete rest. This is the energy necessary to sustain life.

BMR is influenced by a number of factors, one of which is body size and composition. Large individuals have higher BMR's than small individuals, because they have more cells that utilize calories. Another influencing factor is age. The BMR declines with age at approximately 2 percent per decade after twenty-five years of age. This means if your diet remains constant, you will gain a considerable amount of weight as you grow older. For example, pretend you are twenty-five years old and in perfect caloric balance at 154 pounds eating 2,800 calories a day. If you continue to eat the same amount (2,800 calories a day) until you reach seventy-five years, you will gradually gain until at age seventy-five you would weigh 279 pounds. You must reduce your caloric intake as you get older.

Another influencing factor of BMR is that women on the average have a 10 percent slower BMR than men. This means it is easier for women to gain weight than men. Therefore, women must be ever conscious of their caloric intake.

There are other factors that influence weight control such as hormonal secretions to the thyroid gland, heredity, and abnormal digestive systems. With so many factors influencing weight control, it is understandable why people vary in weight control and why some people can eat almost anything and never gain weight or vice versa.

Now that we have a clearer understanding of factors that influence weight control, let us turn our attention to the formula for losing weight. A knowledge of the principles involved in this formula will enable us to make some rational decisions about losing weight.

Weight Loss Formula

Caloric Balance = Calories from food
$-$ [calories from basal metabolic rate
$+$ calories from work metabolism
$+$ calories lost in excretion]

Caloric balance occurs when the calories taken in equal those expended.

Calories from food means the total number of calories taken into the body.

Calories from BMR are those calories utilized while at complete rest.

Calories from work metabolism means the calories that are utilized during physical exertion.

Calories lost in excretion are those calories not digested from food.

If you are satisfied with your percentage of body fat and body weight, you should strive for caloric balance. This means your daily caloric input should equal your daily caloric output. Because the only way calories can enter the body is through the consumption of food, the type and quantity of food consumed determine the total number of calories that enter the body.

Calories leave the body in three ways. First, calories are burned up by our BMR. Second, calories are burned up by our daily physical exertion. Third, some calories are lost through excretion of food that is not digested as energy. Let us analyze each part of the formula and determine how to lose weight.

Calories from Food

If you plan to lose weight, reduce the amount of calories consumed without sacrificing the basic nutritional needs such as vitamins, minerals, and proteins. Select a variety of foods low in calories from table 5.7 and begin a moderate diet. Do not go on a crash diet or eat fewer calories than needed for your BMR. A crash diet can harm your body's metabolism. Try to eat three small, well-balanced, low-calorie meals daily.

Calories from BMR

The BMR depends on several factors such as age, body size, gender, and function of the endocrine glands. Precise measurements of the BMR requires a trained specialist using special equipment. Exercise physiologists have developed a simpler, fairly accurate procedure for calculating the BMR, provided there are no endocrine or hormonal abnormalities.

One kilogram (2.2 pounds) of body weight burns approximately one calorie per hour in a male between fifteen and twenty-five years of age. In women of the same age, one kilogram of body weight burns approximately 0.9 calories per hour. As mentioned, age and body size also affect the BMR. As you get older, your BMR decreases in the number of calories used daily. BMR also decreases with a smaller body size. Women have approximately a 10 percent reduction in the BMR.

To determine your BMR, first divide your weight by 2.2 to determine your weight in kilograms. Second, obtain from table 5.5 your caloric per kilogram of body weight at your particular age. Now multiply your body weight in kilograms by your age adjustment figure. The results show your BMR for one hour. To determine your BMR for twenty-four hours, multiply your one-hour BMR by twenty-four. For example, compare the BMR for two women, ages sixty and twenty, who both weigh 132 pounds.

Sixty-year-old woman	Twenty-year-old woman
60 weight in kilograms 2.2)132.0 weight in pounds	60 kilograms 2.2)132.0 pounds
60 kilograms ×.7 age adjustment 42.0 calories per hour ×24 hours in day 1008 calories BMR for 24 hours	60 kilograms ×.9 age adjustment 54 calories per hour ×24 hours in day 1296 calories BMR for 24 hours

As you can see, the sixty-year old woman cannot eat as much food as the twenty-year old woman and expect to keep her weight down. If the older woman consumed a hamburger, french fries, and a soft drink, she would nearly equal her BMR for the day. As can be seen, it is easy to gain weight as you get older, which makes it imperative to eat less or exercise more to burn up excess calories as you age.

Table 5.5
Determination of Age Adjustment for Men and Women in BMR

Age	Men's Age Adjustment (Cal/Kg body wt)	Women's Age Adjustment (Cal/Kg body wt)
15-25	1.00	0.9
26-35	0.95	0.85
36-45	0.9	0.8
46-55	0.85	0.75
56-65	0.8	0.7
65 and over	0.75	0.65

Calories from Work Metabolism

Daily caloric expenditures vary widely because of differences in job requirements and recreational endeavors. The harder the physical work, the more calories expanded. It would be impractical to try to calculate your caloric expenditures exactly for the whole day, because you constantly change your activity level. Exercise physiologists have devised a method to estimate the calories you expend during a twenty-four-hour period.

First, determine the activity intensity level that best describes your daily activity from table 5.6. After you have chosen your activity intensity level, multiply that percentage by your BMR for twenty-four hours, then add the result to your BMR. For example, to calculate the calories expended for the sixty- and twenty-year-old woman described earlier, multiply each woman's BMR by, say, 60 percent (intensity level) to determine the calories expended during physical activity. Then add the results to their BMR.

Sixty-year-old woman		**Twenty-year-old woman**	
1,008	BMR	1,296	BMR
×0.60	activity intensity level	×0.60	activity intensity level
604.80	calories expended for physical activity	777.60	calories expended for physical activity
1,008	BMR	1,296	BMR
+605	calories needed for activity	+778	calories needed for activity
1,613	calories expended in one day	2,074	calories expended in one day

The sixty-year-old woman needs to consume approximately 1,613 calories a day to maintain her body weight, whereas, the twenty-year-old woman needs to consume nearly 2,074 calories a day. If they consume more calories than they expend, they will gain weight. If they consume less calories, they will lose weight.

Table 5.6
Activity Intensity Levels for Men and Women

Intensity level %	Classification
40	Sedentary—very limited physical activity. Limited to walking and sitting (office workers, teachers, clergymen, etc.)
50	Semisedentary—engaged in activities that involved standing and walking (policeman, housework, foreman, etc.)
60	Laborers—manual physical work (lifting, pushing etc.) Also includes light calisthenics, walking or jogging a mile, etc.
70	Heavy workers—regular participation in vigorous physical activity (racquetball, tennis, swimming, running, weight training, etc.)
80	Athletic training—marathon running, swimming and bicycling long distances, intercollegiate sports. Very vigorous daily physical fitness program.

Research has found that approximately 100 calories are burned up for every mile one covers in physical activity. For example, nearly 100 calories are burned up whether you walk a fifteen-minute mile or run a seven-minute mile. It is advisable to burn up at least 300-400 calories a day through physical exercise. If you are a walker, then walk three miles a day. If you are a jogger, then jog three miles a day. Not only will this physical activity help you to lose or maintain body weight, but also help improve your cardiovascular system.

Calories Lost in Excretion

A certain number of calories are not consumed in digestion and are excreted as waste materials. Each individual is different in the amount of calories excreted. Most medical authorities estimate that the average individual loses approximately 5 percent of the calories consumed through excretion. Therefore, if you consume 2,000 calories daily, then you will excrete approximately 100 calories (5 percent of 2000).

Now that we have analyzed the formula, let us calculate our caloric consumption and plan to lose weight. Use the example of the sixty- and twenty-year-old women who both weigh 132 pounds (60 kilograms) and eat approximately 1,800 calories daily. Substitute what we know about these women in the formula.

Sixty-Year-Old Woman

Caloric Balance = Calories from food − [calories from basal metabolic rate + calories from work metabolism + calories lost in excretion]
= 1,800 − (1,008) (BMR) + 605 (work) + 90 (5% of 1,800)
= 1,800 − 1,703
= + 97 calories a day

Twenty-Year-Old Woman

Caloric Balance = Calories from food − [calories from BMR + calories from work metabolism + calories lost in excretion]
= 1,800 − (1,296) (BMR) + 778 (work) + 95% of 1,800
= 1,800 − 2,164
= − 364 calories a day

Nutritionists tell us that to lose one pound of fat tissue, we must create a deficit of 3,500 calories between calories consumed and expended. So if we divide each woman's difference in calories consumed with calories expended, then we can see that the sixty-year-old woman will gain one pound of fat tissue (3500 ÷ 97) approximately every thirty-six days or about ten pounds in a year. The twenty-year-old woman will lose one pound of fat tissue (3500 ÷ 364) nearly every 9.6 days or about thirty-eight pounds a year.

Let us see how much weight the sixty-year-old woman

could lose if she went to a moderate diet of 1,200 calories daily and increased her activity level to 70 percent.

Caloric balance = 1,200 calories − (1,008) BMR + 706 (70% level)
+ 60 (5% of 1,200)
= 1,200 − 1,774
= −774 calories a day

If we divide 774 calories into 3,500 calories (needed to lose one pound), then we can see that this woman will lose one pound of fat approximately every four and one-half days. So the best way to lose weight is to moderately reduce your caloric intake and increase your physical activity until you reach your desired weight. Try not to lose more than two pounds a week because your metabolism could be harmed from such a drastic change in weight. *Never* go on crash diets and consume less calories than your *BMR,* for research indicates that you can permanently lower your BMR because the body will protect itself by lowering the BMR to conserve the body's glucose. Also the weight that you lose will not be all fatty tissue but lean muscle tissue.

If you permanently lower your BMR, then weight gain will be harder to arrest. I often read about diets that advocate severe restrictions on caloric intake (some as low as 300 calories a day). I do not recommend participation in these diet plans, for the health consequences should be of greater concern to you than the fast weight loss. Calculate your BMR and set this as the lower limit for your caloric restrictions. Also increase your work output through physical activity.

Substitute your physical dimensions into the formula to determine whether you are maintaining or losing weight. Remember, if you expend more calories than you consume, you will lose weight and show honor and glory to God's temple.

What Can I Eat?

Recently, after a physical-fitness seminar that I was conducting in a church, a confused lady asked me, "With all the various contradictions concerning what food is harmful or good for you, what can I eat?" Her bewilderment is justified for there seems to be confusion in our literature about the nature of our foods that we are eating.

With her question in mind, a list of foods were analyzed and given points according to their nutritional value. The higher the points, the more nutritious the food. Points have been given foods for their content of protein, dietary fiber, naturally occurring sugars and starch, polyunsaturated fat, vitamins, and two minerals (iron and calcium). On the other hand, points were deducted for total fat content (saturated and monounsaturated), cholesterol, sodium, and added sugars. Points were not given according to calories in the food. If you want to go on a diet, choose those nutritional foods low in calories.

The formulas used to score these foods reflect current scientific beliefs about nutrition and health. A diet high in saturated fat and cholesterol greatly increases the risk of coronary heart disease. Low-fiber diets enhance the risk of colon cancer. An abundance of salt (sodium) in the diet promotes high blood pressure. Refined sugar promotes obesity, diabetes, hypoglycemia, and tooth decay.

Choose foods near the top of the table with positive values, and eat fewer of the foods with negative values or that are near the bottom of the table. Try to eat a varied diet composed mainly of grains and grain products (high in fiber), lean meats, dried beans and nuts, fresh vegetables, fruits, poultry and fish, and low-fat dairy products.

Ratings listed are for average size servings. Adjust the score proportionately for larger or smaller portions. Rating of different items can be added together. For example, pancakes and syrup have a score of twenty-five. (Four pancakes are plus thirty-one points; pancake syrup is minus six points.) While the rating may be added, no absolute goal must be reached each day, although it is recommended that between 400 and 500 positive points be accumulated a day.

Table 5.7 Nutritional Scoreboard

VEGETABLES

Most vegetables are great sources of vitamins, especially A and C, and minerals and usually taste best either raw or just lightly cooked.

		Points	Kcal
spinach, fresh	2 cups, raw	91	80
collard greens, fresh	½ cup, cooked	90	18
sweet potato	1 med., baked	82	295
potato	1 med., baked	71	90
kale, fresh	½ cup, cooked	71	15
winter squash (acorn, butternut)	½ cup, baked	70	65
broccoli, fresh	½ cup, cooked	68	20
asparagus, fresh	½ cup, cooked	67	15
spinach, frozen	½ cup, cooked	65	20
mixed vegetables, frozen	½ cup, cooked	63	35
broccoli, frozen	½ cup, cooked	59	25
brussel sprouts, fresh	½ cup, cooked	58	25
tomato	1 medium	56	40
rutabaga	½ cup, cooked	54	25
lima beans, frozen	½ cup, cooked	53	95
green peas, frozen	½ cup, cooked	45	58
sweet corn, fresh (on-the-cob)	1 ear, cooked	41	70
cauliflower, fresh	½ cup, raw	36	13
cabbage, chopped	1 cup, raw	36	10
okra	½ cup, cooked	34	13
yellow corn, canned*	½ cup, drained	34	85
sweet peas, canned*	½ cup, drained	33	58
asparagus, canned*	½ cup, cooked	23	15
artichoke, fresh	½ bud	23	45
green beans, fresh	½ cup, cooked	22	95
summer squash (zucchini)	½ cup, cooked	22	15
turnips	½ cup, cooked	21	15
potatoes, French fried	10	19	155
bean sprouts, mung	½ cup	18	18
eggplant	4 oz	18	189
lettuce, romaine	1 cup	17	15
green beans, canned*	½ cup, drained	17	15
sauerkraut*	½ cup, drained	14	25
onion, chopped	¼ cup, raw	12	40
lettuce, iceberg	1 head	11	60
mushrooms, fresh	¼ cup, raw	9	20
avocado†	½ medium	6	185

*All canned vegetables are high in salt.
†Avocado is the only high-fat vegetable.

Table 5.7 Continued

FRUITS

Fruits give natural sweetness, fiber, and a wide variety of minerals and vitamins, especially A and C.

		Points	Kcal
watermelon	10x1 in. slice	68	115
papaya	½ medium	60	35
cantaloupe	¼ medium	60	60
mango	½ medium	52	90
orange	1 medium	49	65
grapefruit	½ medium	42	45
banana	1 medium	36	100
honeydew melon	7x2 in. slice	35	31
strawberries	½ cup	34	30
pear	1 medium	29	100
raspberries	½ cup	27	35
peach	1 medium	26	35
prunes, uncooked	3 medium	26	90
tangerine	1 medium	26	40
apple	1 medium	23	70
blueberries	½ cup	21	45
pineapple, fresh	½ cup	18	35
cherries	½ cup	17	40
pomegranate	½ fruit	14	80
plum, red	1 medium	12	25
grapes	½ cup	10	95

BEVERAGES

Most beverages made from fruits and vegetables are high in vitamins A and C and natural sugars; they also contain modest amounts of other vitamins and minerals. While some low-scoring beverages may be fortified with one or two vitamins, they are all high in added sugar (or contain saccharin).

		Points	Kcal
carrot juice	6 oz	43	23
orange juice, unsweetened	6 oz	47	82
tomato juice	6 oz	36	35
grapefruit juice, unsweetened	6 oz	36	48
V-8 juice	6 oz	26	35
apple juice	6 oz	23	60
grape juice, frozen	6 oz	15	99
pineapple-grapefruit juice	6 oz	11	95
coffee or tea‡	6 oz	00	2
Tab, other diet sodas+	12 oz, 1 can	− 1	1
Cranberry Juice Cocktail	6 oz	− 6	131
Awake	6 oz	− 8	88
Tang	6 oz	− 9	64
Hawaiian Punch	6 oz	−13	87
Hi-C	6 oz	−15	93

Table 5.7 Continued

BEVERAGES

		Points	Kcal
Welchade Grape Drink	6 oz	− 19	100
lemonade	6 oz	− 20	89
Kool-Aid, presweetened	6 oz	− 21	90
Gatorade	12 oz, 1 can	− 34	62
Coca-Cola, other sodas‡	12 oz, 1 can	− 55	144

‡Scientific studies indicate that moderate amounts of caffeine can cause birth defects and other reproductive problems. Pregnant women should minimize their intake of coffee, tea, and caffeine-containing soft drinks.
+Diet sodas contain saccharin, an artificial sweetener that may cause cancer.

POULTRY, FISH, MEAT, AND EGGS

Lower-scoring foods tend to be high in calories (eggs), fat (red meat), or sodium (processed meats). Foods near the top are excellent sources of iron, protein, and other nutrients. Red meat scores are for cooked, semi-trimmed cuts. (If more than half the removable fat is trimmed away, scores improve; if less than half is removed, scores fall.) Next time instead of frying these foods, try baking, broiling, or poaching them.

		Points	Kcal
beef liver, fried^{ll}	3 oz	119	130
chicken livers, simmered^{ll}	2 livers, (1.8 oz)	90	157
tuna, waterpack	3 oz	75	118
lobster, cooked meat	3 oz	72	138
chicken, roasted, skinless	3 oz	68	115
salmon, pink, fillet	7¾ oz can	67	277
turkey, roasted	3 oz	62	210
flounder, baked	3 oz	54	173
scallops, steamed	3 oz	52	85
salmon, sockeye red, canned	7¾ oz can	52	330
round steak	3 oz	51	222
cod, broiled	3 oz	50	144
crabs, steamed meat	3 oz (1 cup)	46	76
veal cutlet, broiled	3 oz	44	184
clams, raw or steamed	5 clams (2.5 oz)	43	50
chicken, roasted with skin	3 oz	42	125
shrimp, steamed	3 oz	42	100
tuna, oilpack, drained	3 oz	40	170
leg of lamb	3 oz	34	237
shrimp, breaded, fried	3 oz	31	160
ham, baked□	3 oz	28	200
chicken, breaded, fried	2 oz (1 thigh)	27	90
rump roast	3 oz	26	295
pork chop, baked	3 oz	25	230
Canadian-style bacon□	2 slices (2 oz)	21	67
sirloin steak	3 oz	17	330
hamburger, 20% fat, lean	3 oz	14	245
ham, smoked□	2 slices (2 oz)	12	163

Table 5.7 Continued

POULTRY, FISH, MEAT, AND EGGS

		Points	Kcal
egg white	1 large	11	17
hamburger, 25% fat, regular	3 oz	− 4	275
bacon□	2 slices (½ oz)	− 5	90
egg, hard boiled	1 large	− 7	81
hard salami□	2 oz	−18	254
pork sausage	3 links (2 oz)	−19	231
hot dog□	1 (1.5 oz)	−20	105
beef bologna□	2 slices (2 oz)	−26	190
luncheon meat□	2 slices (2 oz)	−33	196
Spam□	3 oz	−35	264

ᴵᴵLiver is rich in iron, protein, trace minerals, and numerous vitamins, and is low in fat. However, it is high in cholesterol and may be contaminated with pollutants. Eat liver only occasionally.
□These meats contain sodium nitrite, an additive that can react with other chemicals to form a cancer-causing nitrosamine.

DAIRY

The best dairy foods are lowfat milks, yogurts, and cottage cheeses. While all are good sources of protein, calcium, and riboflavin, the lower-scoring foods are high in saturated fat and sodium.

		Points	Kcal
yogurt, lowfat, plain	8 oz, 1 cup	64	150
skim milk	8 oz	55	130
buttermilk, 1% fat	8 oz	46	110
lowfat milk, 2% fat	8 oz	43	90
cottage cheese, 1% fat	½ cup	30	35
whole milk	8 oz	28	150
chocolate milk, 2% fat	8 oz	27	190
ricotta cheese, part skim	½ cup	26	123
lowfat American cheese	2 oz	26	95
mozzarella cheese, part skim	2 oz	19	180
cottage cheese, 4% fat	2 oz	17	80
yogurt, lowfat, fruit	8 oz, 1 cup	10	150
ricotta cheese, whole milk	½ cup	− 1	130
mozzarella cheese, whole milk	2 oz	− 1	290
cheddar cheese	2 oz	−10	180
cream cheese	½ oz, 1 cubic in.	−11	60
American cheese	2 oz	−18	226

CONDIMENTS

Go easy on condiments, which can easily add unwanted salt, fat, or sugar to your diet.

		Points	Kcal
tomato sauce	¼ cup	13	55
molasses	1 tbsp	2	33
low-calorie Italian salad dressing	1 tbsp	0	18

Table 5.7 Continued

CONDIMENTS

		Points	Kcal
catsup	1 tbsp	– 1	24
soy sauce	1 tbsp	– 2	11
cream, half and half	1 tbsp	– 2	22
mayonnaise, imitation	1 tsp	– 3	26
margarine, diet	1 tbsp	– 3	50
safflower oil	1 tsp	– 3	45
whipped cream	1 tbsp	– 3	45
sour cream	1 tbsp	– 4	28
coffee whitener	1 tbsp	– 5	8
margarine, soft	1 tbsp	– 5	101
Cool Whip	1 tbsp	– 5	14
mayonnaise	1 tbsp	– 6	105
pancake syrup	1 tbsp	– 6	54
margarine, stick	1 pat	– 6	36
French salad dressing	1 tbsp	– 6	56
cream, light	1 tbsp	– 6	45
sugar	1 tbsp	– 6	46
honey**	1 tbsp	– 7	61
cranberry sauce	1 tbsp	– 7	33
blue cheese salad dressing	1 tbsp	–12	70
butter	1 pat	–13	35

**Honey is essentially an unprocessed sugar and contains insignificant amounts of nutrients. Both honey and sugar promote tooth decay.

GRAIN FOODS

Contrary to a widespread myth, starchy grain foods are not fattening. Most people would do well to eat more grain foods in place of meat. Grains, especially whole grains, are a nicely balanced, lowfat source of carbohydrates, vitamins, and protein.

		Points	Kcal
bulgar (cracked wheat)	½ cup, cooked	77	104
whole wheat pita (Syrian) bread	1 pouch	73	115
whole wheat bread	2 slices	55	108
brown rice	½ cup, cooked	47	100
rye bread	2 slices	46	120
white bread, enriched	2 slices	45	140
white rice, enriched	½ cup, cooked	45	110
pearled barley	½ cup, cooked	42	173
corn bread	2-in. square	38	130
white rice, enriched, instant	½ cup, cooked	36	140
spaghetti, enriched	1 cup, cooked	32	216
macaroni, enriched	1 cup, cooked	32	192
pancakes, buckwheat (mix)	four 4-in. cakes	31	280
oatmeal	½ cup, cooked	30	105
wheat germ	2 tbsp	24	30
hominy grits	½ cup, cooked	23	70

Table 5.7 Continued

BEANS, NUTS, AND SEEDS

Beans, nuts, and seeds are excellent sources of dietary fiber, protein, vitamins, and minerals. Beans are generally low in fat; peanuts and most nuts and seeds are high in both fat and calories.

		Points	Kcal
black beans	½ cup, cooked	93	90
chickpeas (garbanzo beans)	½ cup, cooked	90	92
lima beans	½ cup, cooked	73	94
navy beans	½ cup, cooked	61	96
lentils	½ cup, cooked	57	105
kidney beans	½ cup, cooked	56	115
split beans	½ cup, cooked	51	145
black-eyed peas	½ cup, cooked	49	95
soybeans	½ cup, cooked	46	139
tofu (bean curd)	1 piece, 4 oz, 2½x2¾x1 in.	31	88
sunflower seeds, hulled	1 oz	24	86
almonds, shelled	1 oz	18	170
peanuts, roasted	1 oz	11	176
cashews	1 oz	7	173
peanut butter	2 tbsp	5	200
English walnuts	1 cup	3	679
sesame seeds	1 tsp	2	9

BREAKFAST CEREALS

The best cereals are whole grain and relatively unprocessed. Among processed cereals look for whole grain, low sugar content, and no artificial colorings and flavorings. Companies have fortified many cereals with vitamins and minerals in part to distract attention from the products' high sugar contents. Most cereal boxes now declare "grams of added sugar" on the side panel. Because the Nutrition Scoreboard system is not designed to handle fortifications equivalent to vitamin pills, the figures below indicate percentage of sugar by weight (including all naturally occurring sugars). (Figures from U.S. Department of Agriculture.) Better choices are indicated in italics.

	% Sugar by Weight	Quantity	Kcal
Wheat germ	0	¼ cup	110
Oatmeal	0	⅔ cup	107
Farina	0	¼ cup	156
Wheatena	0	¼ cup	110
Puffed wheat or *rice*	0	1 oz	96
Shredded Wheat	1	⅔ cup	110
Cheerios	3	1 oz	110
Wheat-Chex, Corn-Chex, Rice-Chex	4	1 cup	110
Kix	5	1½ cup	110
corn flakes	5	1 cup	110

Table 5.7 Continued

BREAKFAST CEREALS

	% Sugar by Weight	Quantity	Kcal
Special K	5	1¼ cup	110
Grapenuts	7	¾ cup	108
Rice Krispies	8	1 cup	107
Wheaties; Total	8	1 cup	110
Concentrate	9	⅓ cup	110
Product 19	10	1 oz	110
40% Bran	13	⅔ cup	90
Life	16	⅔ cup	105
All Bran	19	⅓ cup	70
100% Bran	21	⅓ cup	70
Quaker 100%	21	⅔ cup	107
Frosted Mini-Wheats	26	1 cup	110
C.W. Post	29	¼ cup	131
Raisin Bran	30	¾ cup	120
Golden Grahams	30	1 cup	110
Cocoa Puffs	33	1 oz	110
Trix	36	1 cup	110
Honey Comb	37	1⅓ cup	113
Alpha Bits	38	1 cup	173
Count Chocula	40	1 oz	110
Cap'n Crunch	40	¾ cup	121
Crazy Cow	40	1 cup	110
Sugar Frosted Flakes	41	⅔ cup	110
Lucky Charms	42	1 cup	110
Cocoa Fruity Pebbles	42	⅞ cup	117
Cookie Crisp, vanilla	44	1 cup	110
Frankenberry	44	1 cup	110
Super Sugar Crisp	46	⅞ cup	113
Fruit Loops	48	1 cup	110
Apple Jacks	55	1 cup	110
Sugar Smacks	56	1 cup	110

SNACKS

Most packaged chips and similar snacks add salt, calories, and questionable preservatives to the diet. Crisp raw vegetables, fresh fruit, and moderate amounts of nuts and seeds make great snacks.

		Points	Kcal
carrot	1 medium	48	21
green pepper	½ cup	44	13
dried apricots††	¼ cup	31	140
raisins††	1 box (1.5 oz)	28	250
soynuts, salted	1 oz	28	139
apple	1 medium	23	66
pretzels, 3-ringed	3 pretzels	19	150

103

Table 5.7 Continued

SNACKS

		Points	Kcal
popcorn, plain	1 cup	19	57
celery	four 5-in. pieces	17	30
Ry-Krisp	2 triple crackers	17	60
potato chips	1 oz	15	150
corn chips	1 oz	13	160
graham crackers	2 crackers, 2½-in. square	12	56
saltine crackers	4 crackers	10	64
jumbo peanuts (in the shell)	10	9	140
popcorn, butter and salt	2 cups	6	114
Cheez-its	10 crackers	5	115
Pringle's potato chips	1 oz	4	157
dill pickle	1 medium	− 3	8
sugar wafers	2	− 3	98
Popsicle	1	−27	70
marshmallows	4	−28	62
Hostess Twinkies	1 piece	−34	130
Hunt's Vanilla Snack Pack Pudding	1 can, 5 oz	−34	190
jellybeans	10	−38	105
Hershey's milk chocolate	1 bar (1.5 oz)	−42	197

††Natural sugars in dried fruit are sticky and can promote tooth decay.

DESSERTS
Most desserts are high in fat, sugar, and calories.

		Points	Kcal
cantaloupe	¼ medium	60	60
strawberries	½ cup	34	30
applesauce, unsweetened	½ cup	17	54
pineapple, canned in juice	½ cup	17	92
muffin, blueberry	1 muffin	8	140
ice milk, vanilla	¼ pint	7	100
frozen yogurt, lowfat, vanilla	½ cup	3	150
frozen yogurt, lowfat, fruit	½ cup	− 1	160
cake, angelfood	1 med. slice	− 1	108
sherbet, orange	½ cup	− 2	150
pudding, chocolate	½ cup	− 7	205
pears, heavy syrup	½ cup	− 8	94
cake, sponge	1 med. slice	−10	190
peaches, heavy syrup	½ cup	−10	102
applesauce, sweetened	½ cup	−10	91
brownies, nut	1¾-in. square	−12	80
apple pie a la mode	med. slice with small scoop ice cream	−15	350
cupcake, plain	1	−16	130
pound cake, old-fashioned	1 med. slice	−18	200
ice cream, vanilla	1½ cup	−22	150

Table 5.7 Continued

DESSERTS

		Points	Kcal
Jell-O, flavored	½ cup	−26	80
Sara Lee chocolate cake, frozen	1 med. slice	−27	185
chocolate eclair	1	−30	275

Adapted from *Nutritional Scoreboard* by Katherine Kahn, Michael Jacobson, and Jan Zimmerman, which is available from the Center for Science in the Public Interest, 1755 S Street, N.W., Washington, D.C. 20009. Copyright 1980.

Eat a Variety of Foods!

Now that you have learned the nutritional value of foods from table 5.7, let us turn our attention to understanding your daily requirements.

Scientists are not aware of any one "perfect" food that can supply all the recommended daily allowances (RDA's). To meet all our nutritional needs, including those yet to be determined and incorporated into future RDA's, we must eat a variety of foods. The daily food guides thus recommend a large number of nutritious foods, arranged in four broad categories. The four food groups are milk and milk products, meats and meat equivalents, fruits and vegetables, and breads and cereals. Each group contributes a substantial amount of the major nutrients needed for health. The four basic food groups are presented along with daily recommendations for a sound nutritional diet.

1. Milk and milk products (at least two servings daily). This group meets the requirements for calcium, vitamins B_2, B_{12}, and A, a large number of minerals and protein. It is preferable to substitute low-fat milk for whole milk, especially if it is fortified with vitamin D. Homogenized milk is suspected to cause atherosclerosis in some individuals is another reason why you should drink low-fat milk. Foods like cheese, yogurt, cottage cheese, and cream cheese belong in this group.
2. Meat and meat equivalents (at least two servings daily). In general, these two servings of meat provide approx-

imately 50 percent of the protein, 25 percent to 50 percent of the iron, 25 percent to 30 percent of vitamins B_1 and B_2 and 355 of the niacin in the RDA's. Common foods in the meat group are beef, veal, lamb, pork, liver, fish, shellfish, chicken, turkey, ham, navy beans, lima beans, peanuts, peas, eggs, and cheese.

3. Fruits and vegetables (at least four servings daily). Fruits and vegetables are responsible for the major intakes of iron and vitamins A and C; they are good sources of calcium, magnesium, and folic acid. Most fruits and vegetables are nutrients dense, low in calories, low in fat, and high in cellulose or fiber. Because they provide roughage, cellulose, and bulk, the products in this group assure a good intestinal environment. Some of them, such as celery, apples, and carrots, even help clean our teeth.

4. Breads and cereals (at least four servings daily). The major nutrients these foods contribute are calories, iron, niacin, and vitamins B_1 and B_2. Cereals and cereal products include all grains served in whole-grain, enriched, and fortified forms. For example, wheat, corn, oats, potatoes, buckwheat, rice, rye, macaroni, spaghetti, flour, and cornmeal.

To ensure a well-balanced diet, eat a wide variety of foods (with positive points) in the four food groups. Don't just eat from one group (fruits) and skip over the others. Eat in moderation, but do not skip meals. Eat three well-balanced meals daily. Plan your meals wisely, for what you eat will have a definite effect on your health and happiness.

Some Wise Eating Guidelines

Every cell in your body has some basic food requirements. If you lack any of these, your health will be affected. Consequently, an excess of these foods can cause disease such as obesity, kidney disorders, and nutritional disorders. You must maintain a well-balanced diet that contains foods basic to your cell physiology. Incorporate the following guidelines into your daily eating habits.

1. Increase consumption of fruits, vegetables, and whole-grain products.
2. Decrease consumption of refined and processed sugars and foods high in such sugar.
3. Decrease consumption of foods high in total fat and replace with fats obtained from vegetable sources (polyunsaturated).
4. Decrease consumption of animal fat by choosing meats, poultry, and fish with low amounts of saturated fats.
5. Substitute low-fat and nonfat milk for whole milk and low-fat for high-fat dairy products.
6. Decrease consumption of butterfat, meats, and other high-cholesterol sources, especially if you have cholesterol problems.
7. Decrease consumption of salt and foods high in salt content.
8. Drink six to eight glasses of water daily. Restrict use of drinks high in caffeine (coffee, tea, and soft drinks).

These guidelines do not guarantee protection from killer diseases, but do improve protection. A seminary president once remarked that "Christians are literally digging their graves with their teeth." That is a somewhat true statement, for every cell in our body is affected by what we eat or fail to eat. Our dietary habits determine whether we are healthy or sick, happy or unhappy, dead or alive. Yet, many Christians keep pouring abnormally high amounts of junk food, which has no nutritional value to the cell, into their mouths to be ground up by their teeth to be used by their bodies to operate its well-balanced, highly sophisticated, complex bodily functions. When medical complications such as degenerative diseases occur, many Christians either blame God for their affliction, or they cannot believe God would let this happen to them. Scientists estimate that the human body is designed to last approximately 150 years if ideally cared for. Do not blame

God if you destroy his creation by overeating nonnutritional foods. Adhere to these nutritional guidelines. It may take changing your whole life-style, which will be very difficult at first to do. But with good self-discipline and God's help you can change. As Christians, when we show honor to God with our bodies and spirit, it brings us true happiness. Sound nutrition and vigorous exercise can lead to a life-style of quality and happy living.

CHAPTER 6

Happiness Involves Developing Strength and Muscular Endurance

The glory of young men is their strength
(Prov. 20:29).

"Strengthen the weak hands,/and make firm the feeble knees" (Isa. 35:3, RSV). The prophet Isaiah knew the value of a strong body. Yet, many Christians at mentioning the term muscular are immediately turned off to exercise. Senior adults think they are going to break a bone or injure themselves if they weight lift. Women think they will become muscle-bound and lose their femininity. Others don't want to lift weights for fear of becoming so sore that even their hair seems to hurt the day after exercise.

Each one of these excuses are not valid if weight training is done properly. Research has shown that muscles will atrophy (degenerate) if they are not constantly used and strengthened. Senior adults should never just sit in that "rocking chair" for their muscles will deteriorate along with their mobility. Research now shows that weight training causes electrical activity from the nerves to stimulate the growth and strength of bones. This can help prevent osteoporosis (softening of bones), a very prevalent disease in senior adults.

Research has proven that muscular endurance training, if done properly, will not cause bulging muscles in women. In fact, these endurance exercises will actually enhance a woman's appearance. Toning up muscles can reduce the circumference of the upper arms, thighs, and buttocks, thereby helping a woman look more feminine.

For those who fear soreness, weight training—if done on a gradual progression, proper warm-up, and proper stretching—will not cause severe soreness. The problem that causes the greatest amount of soreness is that individuals try to lift too much, too many times, and too often.

Don't use these excuses about weight training, for there are many health benefits received when one has good strength in all one's 600 plus muscles. Let us analyze some of these benefits received from strength training.

Rehabilitate Postural Defects

One of the most important health benefits from muscular training is the rehabilitation of postural defects. As we get older our muscles weaken from disease, causing our skeleton system to deviate from its natural alignment. In many instances, shoulders slump and rotate forward, stomach muscles weaken, and the abdomen protrudes outward. Sometimes the pelvis rotates forward, causing severe lower back pain. Also, the muscles in the hips, legs, and feet weaken, causing the skeletal structure to fall from its natural position, which places pressure on nerves. Therefore, many suffer needlessly from postural deviations that can be prevented throuh proper muscular exercises. Most postural deviations are caused by weak muscles that are unable to properly support the skeletal system. On the other hand some postural deviations are caused by stronger muscles overpulling weaker muscles. For example, in children (especially young girls eleven to fourteen years old) the muscles on their right side may be stronger than those on the left. This can cause their spine to be pulled to the right side, causing the shifting vertebrae to pinch the spinal nerves. This condition, called scoliosis, can lead to paralysis.

Lower Back Pain

Lower back pain ranks second to headache as the most common pain in the United States. If you have the misfortune to suffer from acute lower back pain, you will be joining about 80 percent of the adult population. And half of these will experience a second episode of back pain.

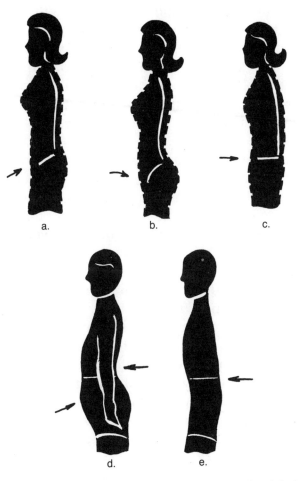

Fig. 6.1 Pelvic Positions: (a) normal, (b) downward pelvic tilt, (c) backward pelvic tilt, (d) ptosis and lordosis, (e) flat back

Lower back pain has many causes. One textbook lists 103 causes. One medical expert states that 90 percent of all patients with lower back pain suffer muscular strain or tearing and accompanying ligament and tendon damage. The remaining 10 percent suffer from congenital (present at birth) defects in the spine, infections, arthritis, or disc problems.

Our sedentary life-style, with help from automated techology, has contributed significantly to lower back pain. Working at a desk job under the stress and strain of a competitive

111

office situation can cause tension, which causes the muscles to remain contracted, causing discomfort.

Many medical authorities believe that emotions, anxiety, tension, and depression are significant factors in at least 80 percent of back problems. These cause our biological fight-or-flight mechanism to pour adrenalin into our system and we become tense and strung out with no release. The end result, backache.

Another cause of lower back pain is overweight. Tremendous stress is borne by muscles and bones carrying extra poundage. Most fat accumulates around the stomach and pelvis. This extra weight causes the pelvis to rotate forward, thus placing extra stress on the vertebrae of the lower back. This condition is known as lordosis or swayback.

The cure of lower back pain lies in therapeutic exercise, including stretching and strengthening routines. For the back that aches because of insufficient activity and loss of muscle tone, appropriate exercise may be the cure. In severe cases, including those resulting from acute injury or surgery, muscle-building exercises can restore a painless back. But these exercises must be repeated daily year after year.

Figures 6.2 to 6.8 show exercises to strengthen and stretch the 140 muscles that support the back. But remember, it takes what no doctor can prescribe—willpower.

Fig. 6.2 Sit-up. Keep knees bent; lift chest to knees; return to floor slowly.

Fig. 6.3a Pull chest to knees.

Fig. 6.3b Touch toes to floor behind head.

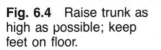

Fig. 6.4 Raise trunk as high as possible; keep feet on floor.

Fig. 6.5 Raise legs as high as possible; keep chin on floor.

Fig. 6.6 Mad cat. Arch back upward; lower as far as possible.

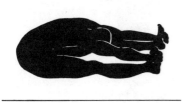

Fig. 6.7 Touch toes; keep legs straight; hold on for eight seconds.

Fig. 6.8 Sit on heels; point toes; lay backward as far as possible.

Neck Joint Disorders

Musculoskeletal disorders in the neck joint are the most common postural deviations, especially among individuals who spend many hours reading or working over a desk. Assuming this posture while working can cause severe headaches. Let us analyze some neck joint disorders.

Forward Head

Forward head (fig. 6.9) often occurs when the muscles in the back of the neck are stretched and weakened, usually because of habitual malposition of the head. Correcting this condition involves aligning the head properly with the chin tucked so that the lower jaw is basically in line with the ground so that the chin is not tipped when the head is drawn back. This requires reorientation of the head and neck so that the individual knows how it feels to hold the head correctly. The head should be held so that the lobe of the ear is in line with the center of the shoulder. The exercises in figures 6.10—6.12 should be beneficial in correcting forward head.

Fig. 6.9 Forward head

Fig. 6.10 Pull forward with arms; push backward with head.

Fig. 6.11 Roll head to side as far as possible.

Fig. 6.12 Roll head in all directions.

a. Normal

b. Forward Head

c. Cervical Lordosis

Fig. 6.13 Cervical lordosis. Notice the abnormal curve in back of neck.

Fig. 6.14 Push backward with arms; push forward with head.

Fig. 6.15a Head tilt

Fig. 15b Head tilt

Fig. 6.16 Push sideways with arms; push opposite direction with head.

Cervical Lordosis

Cervical lordosis (fig. 6.13) may result from an attempt to compensate for other spinal curves occurring lower in the spinal column. Back neck muscles are often tight and contracted so the head is tilted well back and the chin is tipped upward. As in forward head, reeducation of the antagonistic muscles is necessary so that the lower jaw is held in line with the ground. To correct cervical lordosis and forward head, the proper head position must be learned by exercising in front of a mirror to recognize the correct position. The exercise in figures 6.12 and 6.14 should correct cervical lordosis.

Head Tilt or Twist

Looking at the head from the front or back, the head may appear tilted directly to the side and/or with a concomitant twisting of the head and neck (fig. 6.15). In either case, the individual must learn the proper position. Sometimes deviations in the position of the head and neck are compensatory for the postural deviation located below this area. Correction of the head position involves strengthening and shortening the muscles opposite the head tilt, and stretching the muscles toward the head tilt. The exercise in figure 6.12 and 6.16 help eliminate this deviation.

There are many musculoskeletal disorders that occur from weakened muscles, such as scoliosis, kyphosis (humpback), hip, knee, and foot problems. If you suffer from one of these abnormalities, correction and prevention is discussed in detail in several books.[1]

Let's Develop a Weight-Training Program

A basic weight-training program should strengthen all the major muscle groups in a balanced manner. One should never strengthen one part of the body without strengthening other parts equally. Muscle imbalances can cause postural deviations or joint injuries. A knowledge of the proper lifting and breathing techniques is mandatory in order to improve the strength in God's temple. Proper use of weights will increase not only strength and endurance, but also flexibility and power.

Equipment

It doesn't take much equipment or money to get started in a good weight-training program, although using special weight-training machines found in private health clubs makes weight training very convenient. The following equipment can be used to develop a weight-training program at home: steel bar, weight plates, collars, and dumbbells. The steel bar is usually four to six feet long, and weighs about twenty pounds. It has collars at each end which function as protective locks to secure the weight plates on the bar. Weight plates usually come in two and one half-, five-, ten-, and twenty-five-pound increments. Normally, the barbell and collars together weigh about twenty-five pounds. The number of weighted plates needed depends on the type of program. Most adult men need from 175 to 250 pounds of weight for the bar; most women need between 75 to 125 pounds. Dumbbells are end-weighted plates of varying poundages. They are primarily used with one-arm lifts, while the barbell is used for two-arm lifts.

Basic Terms in Weight Training

Weight training has its own unique language and a knowledge of this language helps you understand the techniques of the activity. The term *repetitions* refers to the number of times a complete exercise movement is performed. *Sets* refers to the number of repetitions that are performed. For example, if you lift a barbell ten consecutive times, you have completed one set of ten repetitions. The actual weight or poundage used for an exercise refers to the *load*. The maximum load that can be lifted a given number of times is called *repetitions maximum* (RM). For example, 10 RM is the greatest weight that can be lifted ten times.

Do's and Don'ts in Weight Training

Always follow these important principles and procedures while engaging in a weight training program.

Warm-up.—Whole body warm-up should always precede the regular weight workout. This can be done by jogging slowly or performing light calisthenics until a light sweat appears.

Breathing.—Never hold your breath when performing an extreme effort to overcome heavy resistance. When you hold your breath, it causes the glottis (covering or windpipe) to close. This creates a drastic elevation in thoracic and abdominal pressure. Therefore, you must maintain an open glottis by breathing during an extreme effort. Most weight trainees inhale during exertion and exhale during the relaxation phase.

Starting Loads.—During the first week of training, use lightweight loads to develop the correct form for each exercise and prepare the muscles for the gradual increase in resistance. A weight trainer should lift only the load that can be controlled through a complete range of motion without deviations from the correct form.

Form.—Never sacrifice correct form to lift a heavy weight. Correct form is essential in developing body symmetrically and protecting you from injury.

Range of Motion.—Failure to perform each exercise movement through the complete range of motion will result in only partial development of the primary movers with a corresponding loss of flexibility in the antagonist muscles. This will cause muscle-boundness.

Frequency of Workout.—Normally, you should exercise at least three times per week with a day of rest between each workout. You can work out daily if your exercise routine is alternated between upper and lower body exercises. For the beginner a thirty- to forty-five-minute workout should be sufficient. You may want to lengthen it as strength, endurance, and experience are gained.

Number of Repetitions for Strength.—Between four and six repetitions should be used to develop strength. If you cannot perform an exercise at least four repetitions, then decrease your weight resistance. If you can perform more than six repetitions, then add approximately ten pounds to your total weight resistance. Try to gradually increase until you can do at least three sets per workout period.

Number of Repetitions for Muscular Endurance.—If you desire to primarily gain muscular endurance, then do three sets of ten to twenty repetitions.

Safety Precautions

Improper techniques of lifting can result in injury to yourself or to a training partner. The following hints should be observed:

1. Do not lift more than you can handle with good form. The amount lifted is not important, but rather how well each exercise is performed.
2. Never lift a barbell without collars secured tightly around the weight plates.
3. Make sure the plates are balanced on the barbell.
4. Use chalk or a towel to avoid wet hands caused by perspiration.
5. Always use a spotter when lifting heavy weights to keep from incurring serious injury.
6. Always keep your head up and back straight when lifting. Severe damage can occur to the intervertebral discs of the spinal column if you try lifting with your back bent.
7. Always warm up before lifting.
8. Use rubber-soled shoes to avoid slipping and wear cotton clothing to absorb perspiration.

Basic Weight Training Movements

Muscle contraction causes our body to move in various planes. To strengthen a muscle at a particular joint, you need to know what movement that muscle will cause when it contracts. Kinesiologists (those who study human movement) have given certain terms to describe this joint movement. You need to learn five of these terms to help you understand the muscular training program. All movement terms are made in reference to the human body standing erect, arms hanging to the sides with the palms of the hand turned outward. The five basic movements (fig. 6.17) are as follows:

1. Flexion—bending or decreasing the angle between two bones, for example, bringing the forearm toward the shoulder.
2. Extension—increasing the angle between two bones, for example, returning the forearm to its original straight position.
3. Abduction—moving the bone away from the midline of the body that is drawn to divide the body into right and left halves, for example, raising the arm out to the side of the body.
4. Adduction—moving the bone toward the midline of the body, for example, returning the arm to the side.
5. Circumduction—moving in all planes, for example, rotating the arms in circles.

The following muscular training program is designed to strengthen the basic movements at the major joints in your body. Each exercise is only one example of how to strengthen a certain movement: many exercises can be used. You might even be creative and design some preferred exercises to strengthen the desired movement.

Remember to warm up properly, and also do some stretching exercises before you begin strenuous work. Begin your program by lifting light weights, especially the first three weeks of training. This will reduce much of the soreness that usually accompanies muscular training. Keep a workout record on a chart to help accurately regulate your workouts.

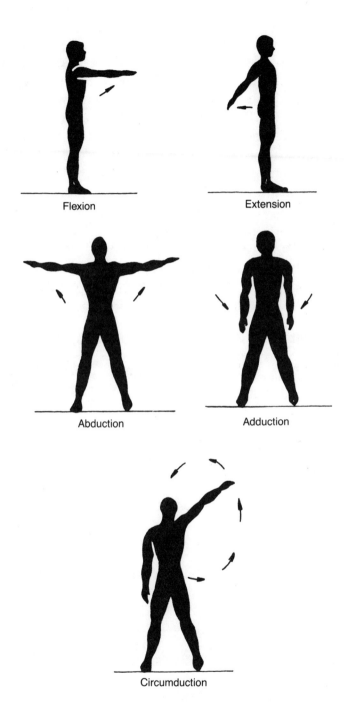

Fig. 6.17   Main movements by the body

Also, avoid doing the same exercise in three consecutive sets. Do one set that works the upper body, then follow this with an exercise that works the lower body. This will eliminate some of the muscular fatigue associated with weight training.

The muscles at these major movements at each joint must be strengthened equally. If a muscle imbalance occurs either from strengthening one muscle group more, or failure to strengthen the muscles at all, then postural deviations are probable. Do strength exercises for each of these movements. If muscle endurance is your goal, then perform from ten to twenty repetitions of each exercise. If strength is your goal, then perform from four to six repetitions of each exercise. The muscular system is an important component of physical fitness that we, as Christians, must develop in order to build God's temple as it was originally designed. (See figs. 6.18—6.49.)

Table 6.1 Basic Weight Training Program

Exercise	Starting Load	Repetitions	Sets
1. Neck			
a. Neck flexion	5 pounds	10-20	1 to 3*
b. Neck extension	5 pounds	10-20	1 to 3
2. Shoulder girdle			
a. Shoulder elevation	25 pounds or 10 RM	10-20	1 to 3
b. Shoulder forward rotation	25 pounds or 10 RM	10-20	1 to 3
c. Shoulder backward rotation	25 pounds or 10 RM	10-20	1 to 3
3. Shoulder joint			
a. Shoulder abduction	10 pounds	10-20	1 to 3
b. Shoulder abduction*		0-20	1 to 3
c. Shoulder flexion	10 pounds	10-20	1 to 3
d. Shoulder extension	10 pounds	10-20	1 to 3
e. Shoulder circumduction	10 pounds	10-20	1 to 3
4. Elbow joint			
a. Elbow flexion	25 pounds	10-20	1 to 3
b. Elbow extension	25 pounds	10-20	1 to 3

5. Wrist joint			
a. Wrist flexion	10 pounds	10-20	1 to 3
b. Wrist extension	10 pounds	10-20	1 to 3
c. Wrist circumduction	10 pounds	10-20	1 to 3
6. Finger and hand joints			
a. Finger flexion	squeeze ball	20-30	1 to 3
7. Upper trunk exercises			
a. Horizontal flexion	50 pounds or 10 RM	10-20	1 to 3
b. Horizontal extension	10 pounds or 10 RM	10-20	1 to 3
8. Lower trunk exercises			
a. Trunk flexion	5 pounds	20-30	1 to 3
b. Trunk extension	5 pounds	20-30	1 to 3
c. Lateral flexion	10 pounds	20-30	1 to 3
9. Hip joint			
a. Hip abduction	5 pounds	10-20	1 to 3
b. Hip adduction	squeeze for 5 secs.	10-20	1 to 3
c. Hip flexion	5 pounds	10-20	1 to 3
d. Hip extension	5 pounds	10-20	1 to 3
10. Knee joint			
a. Knee extension	25 pounds or 10 RM	10-20	1 to 3
b. Knee flexion	10 pounds or 10 RM	10-20	1 to 3
11. Ankle joint			
a. Plantar flexion	50 pounds or 50 RM	10-20	1 to 3
b. Dorsi flexion	5 pounds	10-20	1 to 3

*Begin your weight program with one set. Gradually increase until able to perform three sets.

*If unable to do a chin-up, hold body up as long as possible.

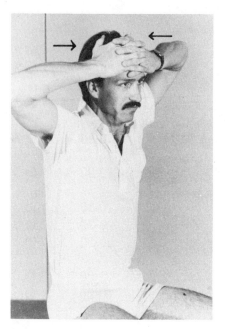

Fig. 6.18 Neck flexion: Push backward with hands; resist with head.

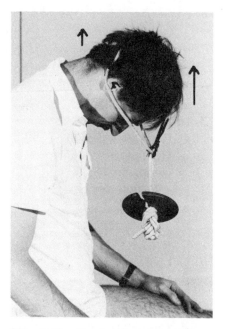

Fig. 6.19 Neck extension: Raise and lower head as far as possible.

Fig. 6.20 Neck Abduction: Press with hands; resist with head.

Fig. 6.21 Shoulder girdle elevation: Keep arms straight; raise and lower shoulders as far as possible.

Fig. 6.22 Shoulder girdle forward rotation: Keep arms straight; rotate shoulders forward as far as possible.

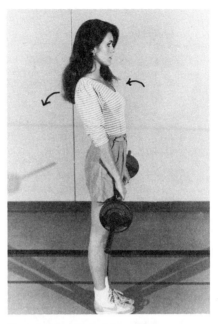

Fig. 6.23 Shoulder girdle backward rotation: rotate shoulders backward; keep arms straight.

Fig. 6.24 Shoulder abduction: Elevate arm upward; keep arm straight.

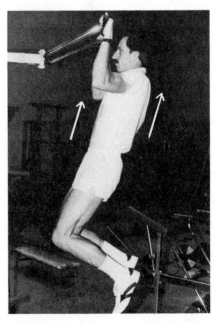

Fig. 6.25 Shoulder abduction: Chin-up; palms outward.

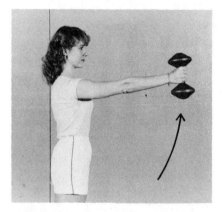

Fig. 6.26 Shoulder flexion: Raise arm upward while keeping arm straight.

Fig. 6.27 Shoulder extension: Raise arm upward and backward with arm straight.

Fig. 6.28 Shoulder circumduction: Circle arm in all directions; keep arm straight.

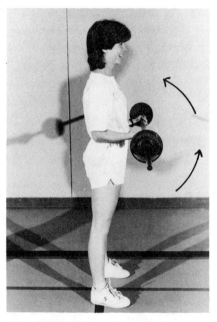

Fig. 6.29 Elbow flexion: Keep back straight; elbows close to side; raise weight upward to chest; lower slowly to legs.

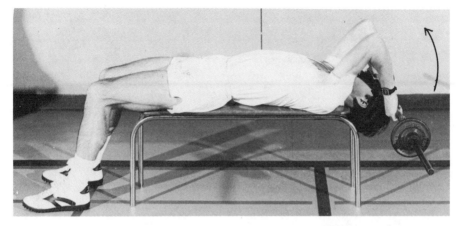

Fig. 6.30 Elbow extension: Keep elbows over ears; straighten arms to full extension; lower slowly.

Fig. 6.31 Wrist flexion: Raise weight upward; lower slowly; palms up; exercise both wrists.

Fig. 6.32 Wrist extension: Reverse grip and extend wrist; lower slowly; exercise both wrists.

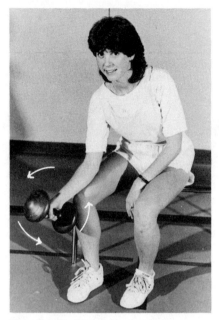

Fig. 6.33 Wrist circumduction: Rotate wrist in all directions; exercise both wrists.

Fig. 6.34 Finger flexion: Squeeze ball tightly; exercise both hands.

Fig. 6.35 Finger extension: Push outwardly with fingers; resist with other hand; exercise both hands.

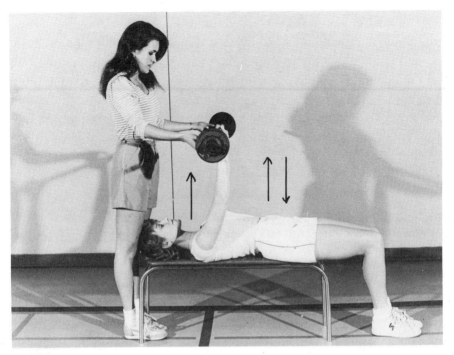

Fig. 6.36 Horizontal flexion bench press: Raise weight upward; lower slowly; acquire a spotter.

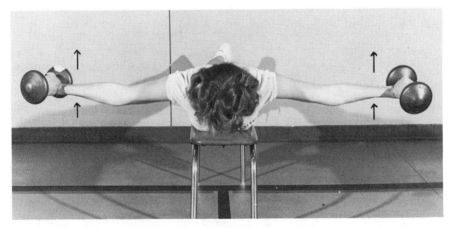

Fig. 6.37 Horizontal extension: Raise weight upward and backward as far as possible; lower slowly.

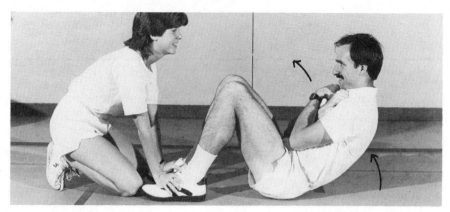

Fig. 6.38 Lower trunk flexion sit-up: Arms on chest; legs bent; raise upward and place chest on legs; lower slowly.

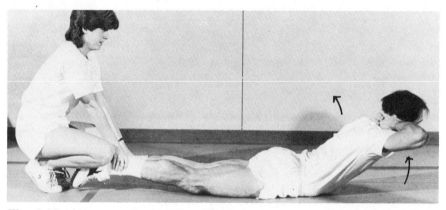

Fig. 6.39 Lower trunk extension: Raise head and trunk backward as far as possible.

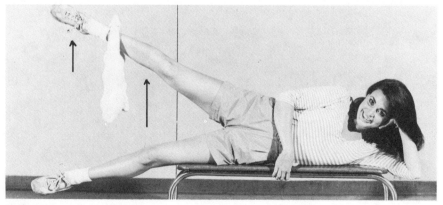

Fig. 6.40 Hip abduction: Raise leg as high as possible; lower slowly; exercise both legs.

Fig. 6.41 Hip abduction: Squeeze legs inward against chair.

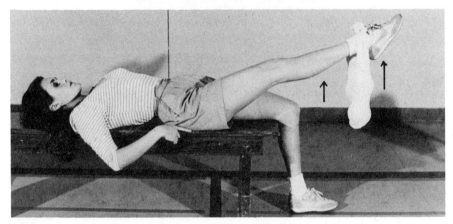

Fig. 6.42 Hip flexion: Keep leg straight; raise weight upward; lower slowly; exercise both legs.

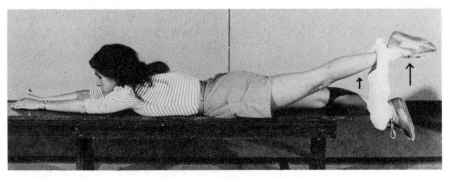

Fig. 6.43 Hip extension: Keep leg straight; raise leg upward as far as possible; lower slowly; exercise both legs.

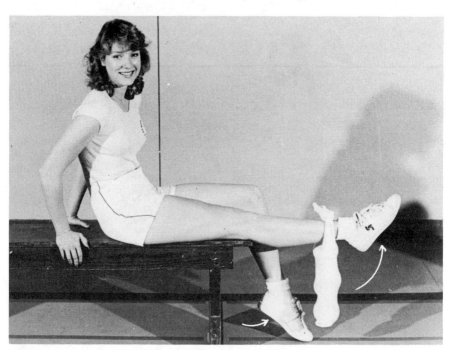

Fig. 6.44 Knee extension: Extend leg until completely straight; lower slowly; exercise both legs.

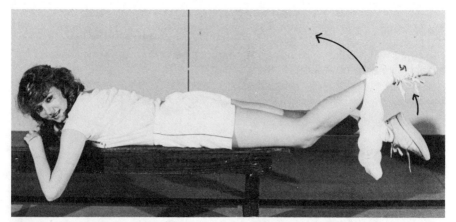

Fig. 6.45 Knee flexion: Raise leg upward; lower slowly; exercise both legs.

Fig. 6.46 Ankle plantar flexion: Raise and lower toes as far as possible.

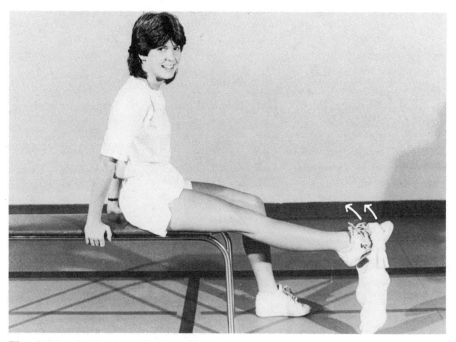

Fig. 6.47 Ankle dorsi flexion: Raise foot toward shin; exercise both legs.

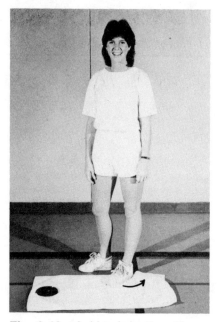

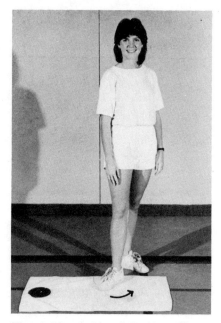

Fig. 6.48 Ankle abduction: Turn foot outward; pull weight toward foot; exercise both feet.

Fig. 6.49 Ankle abduction: Turn foot inward; pull weight toward foot; exercise both feet.

Note

1. Dick Couey, *Building God's Temple* (Minneapolis: Burgess Publishing Company, 1982). H. Falls, A. Baylor, and R. Dishman, *Essentials of Fitness* (Philadelphia: Saunders College, 1980). D. Miller and E. Allen, *Fitness: A Lifetime Commitment* (Minneapolis: Burgess Publishing Company, 1979). K. Wells and K. Luttgens, *Kinesiology* (Philadelphia: W. B. Saunders Company, 1976).

CHAPTER 7
Happiness Involves Developing Flexibility

From whom the whole body, being fitted and held together by that which every joint supplies, according to the proper working of each individual part, causes the growth of the body for the building up of itself in love (Eph. 4:16, NASB).

Several years ago, I attended a physical-fitness seminar that was conducted by an elderly man who challenged all the participants to stand up and touch their toes with their legs straight. To my surprise my fingers barely reached my ankles. It was embarrassing to let this elderly individual show me how inflexible I had become. He also stated that if we couldn't touch our toes with our legs straight we had greatly increased our chances of contracting lower back pain. Since that time, I have always included flexibility in my exercise program.

Flexibility is the quality of being pliant, versatile, and adaptable to change. *Flexibility* is commonly defined as the range of motion about a joint. With age, our bodies tend to become restricted in the actions of bending, stretching, and reaching, which came easily in youth. If we were to return to the school playground and attempt to go through the motions of the past, most of us would be unable to perform the antics and movements of our youth. This is indication enough of our loss of flexibility.

There are many differences in flexibility from one person to the next and within an individual. One contributing factor to the differences within an individual is the type of joint structure. Some people have bone structures that yield greater flexibility. Another potential limiting factor is the amount of muscle and fatty tissue around the joint. A flexibility program, no matter how good, cannot change the basic joint structure. It can, however, stretch the muscles, ligaments, and connective tissue that surround the joint structure.

Fig. 7.1 Some people are more flexible than others.

It is quite easy to conceive a muscle sheath that is seldom stretched beyond its normal resting length becoming so shortened that range of motion is limited. In a flexibility program you must devise a safe means of periodically stretching your muscle and connective tissue. Because flexibility is very specific to the joint involved, no one general exercise can be used. You must select flexibility exercises that will adequately cover the areas of the body needing the exercise.

Flexibility is an important aspect of physical fitness, and the lack of it can create many health disorders. Anyone with a stiff spinal column is susceptible to postural deviations such as lordosis, kyphosis, and scoliosis. Lack of flexibility can also be responsible for muscle injury, compression of nerves, severe headaches, and even some forms of arthritis.

What Type of Stretching Is Best?

The type of stretching movements used in flexibility programs is very important. An understanding of *ballistic* and *static* stretching techniques is necessary before you begin a flexibility program. The trend in safe flexibility programs has been away from ballistic or bouncing-type stretches, where the movement is suddenly and forcefully ended by an abrupt pull on muscle and connective tissue. These types of stretches have been replaced in preference by slow static stretches, where the resistance of the stretch is gradually developed to a point slightly beyond comfort and held for a short time before it is released. Both programs appear to be about equal in the development of flexibility, but the static approach is preferred for several reasons.

First, injuries are reduced, because there is less danger of tearing the connective tissue when the force is gradually applied and held. Second, slow static stretching seems to cause far less muscle soreness than the bouncing-type stretch. In fact, a good way to relieve muscle soreness is by using the slow, gradual static stretch. Third, the stretch receptors (muscle spindles and Gogi tendon organs) located in the muscles and joints are stimulated by specific kinds of stretching movements. These stretch receptors protect the muscles and joints from overstretching and injuring themselves. Using fast, jerky, bouncy movements causes the muscles you are attempting to stretch to contract at the same time. This not only reduces the effectiveness of stretching but also cause muscle soreness. When a slow, sustained stretch is used, the stretch receptors cause the muscle to relax and lengthen, and thus aid in obtaining increased flexibility.

How Flexible Am I?

Every Christian should be able to answer the above question, for it is important to develop flexibility in all your muscles to prevent God's temple from deteriorating. Flexibility is not a

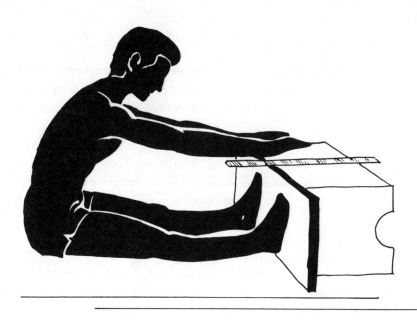

Fig. 7.2a Static stretching. Slowly reach as far as possible.

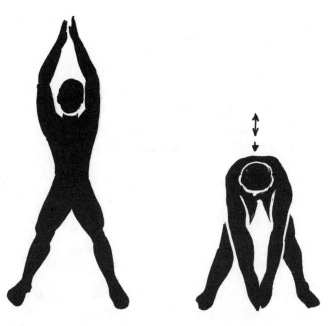

Fig. 7.2b Ballastic stretching; bouncing to reach the floor.

general factor but is specific to each muscle joint. No single test, therefore, can measure the flexibility of all the major joints of the body. The following flexibility tests were chosen to represent the major areas of the body that must remain flexible if good health is desired. Find a partner and determine your flexibility in these important areas.

Lower Back and Hamstrings

The sit-and-reach test (fig. 7.3) measures flexibility of the lower back and hamstring muscles (back of upper leg).

1. Sit on the floor with knees together and feet flat against a bench with a yardstick on top.
2. While a partner holds the knees straight, bend forward and extend both arms and hands as far as possible.
3. Measure the distance on the yardstick from the finger-tips of both hands together to the edge of the bench. If the fingers do not reach the edge, the distance is expressed as a negative score; if they reach beyond the edge, it is expressed as a positive score (table 7.1).

Table 7.1 Flexibility Classifications

Classification	Sit & Reach (in.)	Shoulder Lift (in.)	Trunk Extension (in.)
Men			
Excellent	7 or more	26 or more	23 or more
Good	4-6	23-25	20-22
Average	1-3	20-22	18-19
Below average	0	19 or less	17 or less
Women			
Excellent	8 or more	25 or more	20 or more
Good	5-7	21-24	17-19
Average	2-4	18-20	15-16
Below average	0-1	17 or less	14 or less

Adapted from Miller and Allen, *Fitness: A Lifetime Commitment.*

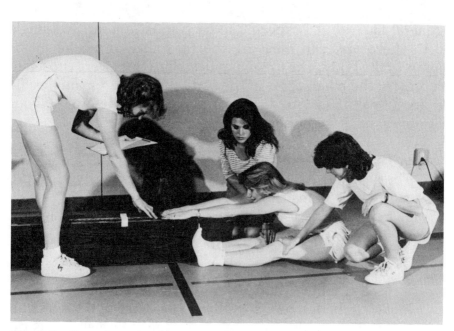

Fig. 7.3 Sit-and-reach test

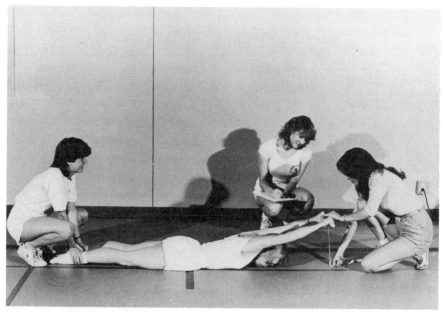

Fig. 7.4 Shoulder lift test

Shoulder Joint and Shoulder Girdle

The shoulder lift test (fig. 7.4) measures flexibility of the shoulder joint and shoulder girdle.

1. Lie prone on the floor. Touch the chin to the floor and extend the arms forward directly in front of the shoulders, grasping the stick at exactly shoulder width apart.
2. Hold the stick horizontally with both hands. Keep the elbows and wrists straight. Watch for bending of the wrist.
3. Raise the arms upward as far as possible while keeping the chin on the floor. Measure the distance in inches from the bottom of the stick to the floor (table 7.2).

Trunk

The trunk extension test (fig. 7.5) measures flexibility of the trunk.

1. Lie prone on the floor with a partner holding the buttocks and legs down.
2. With fingers interlocked behind the neck, raise the chest and head off the floor as far as possible. Measure the distance in inches from the floor to the chin.

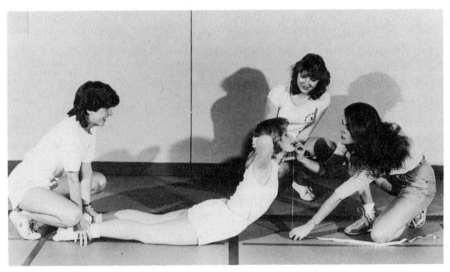

Fig. 7.5 Trunk extension test

Being inflexible in these areas is often a warning signal for lower back problems or tension headaches. If your muscles in these areas are tight and tense, then in all probability your muscles may spasm and cause severe pain. Always maintain good flexibility in these body areas.

How Do I Develop Flexibility?

The following exercises are designed to develop flexibility in the major muscles, joints, and movements of your body. The exercises should be done daily at least five times a week for fifteen to twenty seconds. They should be repeated at least three times. Stretching should never proceed to the point of actual pain and subsequent soreness. There will usually be some discomfort (moderately miserable), but any aftereffects should be noted and given time to repair. Start out easy and slow; do not bounce when you stretch. The following guidelines are recommended.

1. Stretch gently and gradually to prevent soreness and damage to the tissues. Do not bounce.
2. Exercises that do not cause a muscle to lengthen beyond normal may maintain flexibility, but will not increase flexibility. The overload principle also applies to flexibility. To increase flexibility, stretch the muscle beyond its normal length.
3. Perform exercises for each muscle group or joint in which flexibility is desired. Do not skip one group. Maintain a balance program for all muscle groups.
4. Perform flexibility exercises before and after a cardiovascular, respiratory, or strength workout to prevent strains, reduce soreness, and stretch muscles that may have been shortened by the workout. It is important to always perform flexibility exercises both before and after other forms of physical activity.

Fig. 7.6 Posterior neck muscles: Apply light pressure with hands; lower head as far as possible.

Fig. 7.7 Anterior neck muscles: Apply light pressure with hands; extend head as far as possible.

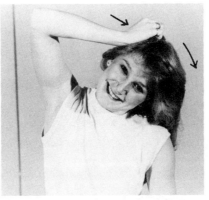

Fig. 7.8 Lateral neck muscles: Apply light pressure to head; lower head to side as far as possible; exercise both sides.

Fig. 7.9 Anterior shoulder muscles: Walk backward with fingers as far as possible. Keep arms spread as little as possible.

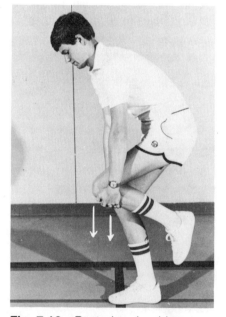

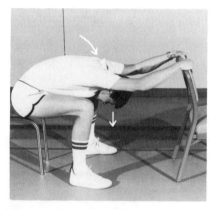

Fig. 7.11 Upper shoulder muscles: Lower body to floor as far as possible.

Fig. 7.10 Posterior shoulder muscles: Push down on hands with knee.

Fig. 7.12 Lower shoulder muscles: Grasp hands behind back; you may need to grasp a towel if unable to grasp hands.

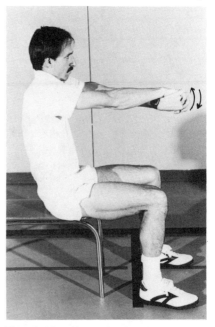

Fig. 7.13 Pronation and supination of arms: Twist to both sides.

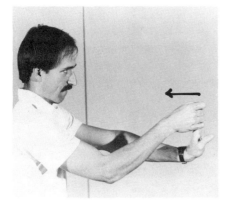

Fig. 7.14 Wrist and finger extension: Pull backward on fingers; exercise both wrists.

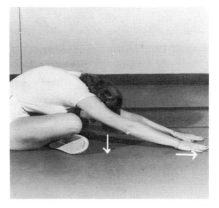

Fig. 7.15 Upper trunk muscles: Reach forward; try to place forehead on floor.

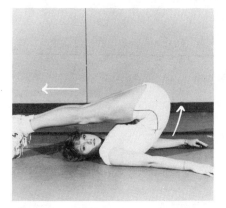

Fig. 7.16 Lower trunk muscles: Try to touch toes behind head; keep legs straight.

Fig. 7.17 Anterior trunk muscles: Slowly allow the weights to pull arms toward floor.

Fig. 7.18 Lateral trunk muscles: Twist as far as possible to both sides.

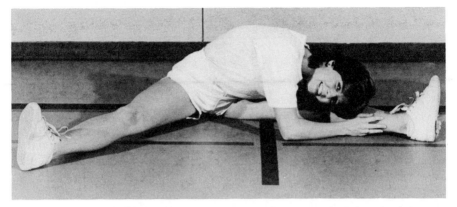

Fig. 7.19 Posterior hip and thigh muscles: Try to put head on both knees; try to place chest on floor in front.

Fig. 7.20 Anterior hip and thigh muscles: Pull legs and chest off floor as far as possible.

Fig. 7.21 Calf muscles: Keep heel on floor; move buttocks toward wall; exercise both calves.

Fig. 7.22 Groin muscles: Push down on legs with elbows.

CHAPTER 8

Happiness Involves Maintaining God's Temple

But they that wait upon the Lord shall renew their strength; they shall mount up with wings as eagles; they shall run, and not be weary; and they shall walk, and not faint (Isa. 40:31).

Exercise and nutrition alone cannot assure a happy and healthy life. There are many Christians who are subjecting themselves to unhealthy stress; many are drinking alcohol while disguising it as social drinking; many are polluting their lungs with poisonous gases, while others upset their body's physiology by taking drugs, either legally or illegally. Proper exercise and nutrition can afford the body better protection against many degenerative diseases but they may be rendered helpless in affording protection to the body if Christians persist in subjecting God's temple to these dangerous stressors. It would be wise for you to examine these stressors and see how they affect his temple. If you do not partake in these stressors, you may want to learn about them so you can witness to your fellow Christians.

Stress

Everybody experiences stress, but no one can quite define it. Stress creates upset stomachs, splitting headaches, intense grief, excessive drinking, and violent arguments. Stress dulls our memories, cripples our thinking, weakens our bodies, upsets our plans, stirs up our emotions, and reduces our efficiency. But stress also motivates us to work, encourages us to keep going when life gets difficult, spurs us to action in the midst of crises, helps us to mature, and, at times, makes life exciting.

Hans Selye, a biologist, describes stress as essentially the

OVER DUE BILLS

Fig. 8.1 How does stress affect you?

wear and tear of living. Each person experiences stress differently, but every day each of us experiences physical and emotional wear and tear from the pressures of life.

According to Selye, stress is not simply nervous tension or something to be avoided nor always unpleasant. Parachute jumping, playing tennis, or watching an emotional television program can all be stressful, but these are stresses that we often seek out and enjoy. When it motivates us to action, stress can be good, but when it places our bodies under prolonged physical and emotional pressure, the very things that might be stimulating and enjoyable become destructive and unpleasant.

Selye believes that just as unused muscles or organs become slack and inefficient, inactivity deprives our bodies and minds of an innate urge to create. He recommends that we be exposed to as many positive stresses as we can handle. As long as we stay within our optimal stress level, our mind and body will be at peak performance.

Trouble starts when too much negative stress occurs, such as pressures at work or school or friction at home. Even good stress can be a problem if there is too much or if we cannot handle it well. If a promotion generates panic, we need to recognize our individual responses to too much stress and not push beyond our endurance. The body sends out warning signals telling us that our system is overloaded and we experience changes in sleep patterns, appetite, sexual desire, or mood.

Stress can cause severe damage to God's temple. Today eight to ten million Americans suffer from ulcers. In fact, tagamet, a drug that helps cure stress and ulcers is the most widely prescribed drug in America. People who suffer from ulcers are usually highly competitive, go-getter men, women, and children. They feel pressure from the world around them, but there is a lot of inner pressure as well. They have an inner drive to succeed and to get ahead. Whenever they accomplish a particular goal, they set their aspirations higher and continue pushing. This keeps the body under such a constant state of physical alertness that the stomach lining begins to bleed and becomes irritated by the increased production of acids. This is the start of an ulcer. The biggest producer of ulcers is stress that cannot be controlled. A person under such stress cannot predict what will happen or make things happen.

Stress not only can bring on ulcers but can also affect the heart. Two cardiologists divided potential heart-attack victims into two broad categories, Type A and Type B. Type A personalities are ambitious, aggressive, self-demanding, competitive, and strive for success. They are driven by the clock. In contrast, Type B personalities are more casual. They are less competitive, less worried about time, and are not unnecessarily preoccupied with achievement. Perhaps no one fits these categories completely, but most of us tend to fall into one of these classifications.

Their research found that persons with Type A personalities were seven times more likely to have a heart attack than Type B individuals. Even if they did not smoke or exercise and had normal blood pressure with no family history of coronary disease, Type A people were more likely to have coronary attacks.

Type A

Type B

Fig. 8.2 Type A and Type B personalities

Stress has also been linked to migraine headaches, arthritis, backaches, and high blood pressure. Some researchers believe that stress can cause certain forms of cancer.

In a study of 450 adult cancer patients, Lawrence LeShan[1] found three prominent characteristics of stress. Most patients experienced termination of a close personal relationship immediately prior to the disease, about half the patients had trouble expressing hostility, and about a third showed tension over death of their parents.

We probably cannot conclude from this and similar research that stress alone causes cancer, heart attacks, or other physical symptoms, but we do know that stress is a key factor in illness, and diseases not caused by stress alone may be influenced by life's pressures. Stress places the body on alert and makes it more susceptible to disease.

In his study of more than 5,000 patients, Holmes discovered that disease often follows any event that requires us to adapt or to change our reactions in some way. He devised a test to measure the influence of change by assigning points to those events that require the greatest adaption to change. Table 8.1 shows these stressors and the points assigned to their degree of stress.

Every reader should check all the items in table 8.1 that have applied to them during the last year. Add up the points to get a total life change unit score. According to Holmes's research, a score less than 150 indicates only one chance in three that you will have a serious change in health during the next two years. A score between 150 and 300 points indicates your chances rise to about 50-50. A score over 300 points indicates an 80 percent chance for a major health change (disease, surgery, accident, mental illness, etc.) within the next two years.

Christian, if stress is prominent in your life, allow your relationship with God to help you overcome tensions, anxieties, and frustrations. Jesus knew the high price of rest when he said in Mark 6:31, "Come ye yourselves apart into a desert place, and rest a while: for there were many coming and going, and they had no leisure so much as to eat."

Table 8.1 The Stress of Adjusting to Change

Rank	Event	Life Change Unit Points
1	Death of spouse	100
2	Divorce	73
3	Marital separation	65
4	Jail term	63
5	Death of close family member	63
6	Personal injury or illness	53
7	Marriage	50
8	Fired at work	47
9	Marital reconciliation	45
10	Retirement	45
11	Change in health of family member	44
12	Pregnancy	40
13	Sex difficulties	39
14	Gain of new family member	39
15	Business readjustment	39
16	Change in financial state	38
17	Death of close friend	37
18	Change to different line of work	36
19	Change in number of arguments with spouse	35
20	Mortage over $10,000	31
21	Foreclosure of mortgage or loan	30
22	Change in responsibilities at work	29
23	Son or daughter leaving home	29
24	Trouble with in-laws	29
25	Outstanding personal achievement	28
26	Wife begins or stops work	26
27	Begin or end school	26
28	Change in living conditions	25
29	Revision of personal habits	24
30	Trouble with boss	23
31	Change in work hours or conditions	20
32	Change in residence	20
33	Change in schools	20
34	Change in recreation	19
35	Change in church activities	19

36	Change in social activities	18
37	Mortgage or loan less than $10,000	17
38	Change in sleeping habits	16
39	Change in number of family get togethers	15
40	Change in eating habits	15
41	Vacation	13
42	Christmas	12
43	Minor violations of the law	11

Reprinted with permission from *Journal of Psychosomatic Research* 11, p. 213-18.

How Do You Overcome Stress?

Most medical authorities recommend the following four ways to cope with stress: Develop a positive mental attitude, (2) practice good nutrition, (3) get proper exercise, and (4) get proper rest and relaxation.

Develop a positive mental attitude.—Understanding stress is the best way to become free from its negative aspects. As with most problem solving, we must first become aware of our particular source of stress before we can reduce or alleviate it.

Try to develop a "I can handle it" attitude. Once we do, we will find that the expectation of coping successfully goes a long way toward actually doing it.

We should also establish priorities to put our problems in perspective. If we feel overworked and that there are not enough hours in a day, we should set schedules based on a clear sense of what can be realistically achieved. This is significant, because only irritation and frustration accompany trying to accomplish things without first assessing our capabilities and planning accordingly. I have seen many Christians mishandle stress because they were unable to budget their time to deal with the complexity of life.

Remember, whether it is stress in your personal or professional life, there will always be some degree of conflict and pressure. If we realize that complete harmony is more an ideal than a reality, we will be able to accept stressful feelings. There is nothing wrong with feeling angry or frustrated if it is properly expressed. In dealing with feelings, though, we must communicate with those around us. Do not be afraid to let people know when you need their help or support; do not expect them to be mindreaders. A little communication does a lot for interpersonal relationships, and many people find that talking about problems can solve them.

Almost any emotional upset can trigger the body's stress response and the accompanying physical effects. When you feel yourself becoming tense, slow down and try to be rational. You may find that some of the things that are most annoying or frustrating just are not worth getting worked up over. It is important to stay happy and healthy, and to remember that worrying over things that cannot be controlled prevents dealing effectively with the things that can be controlled. If you want to be happy and healthy and are willing to work toward it, then chances are you will be.

As Christians, we need to learn to cast our burdens on our Creator and expect that he will sustain and help us, just as the Bible promises. Then the stresses of life will help us grow. They are no longer obstacles to be overcome but steps that enable us to grow to maturity. The positive mental attitude for Christians is found in Philippians 4:13, "I can do all things through Christ which strengtheneth me."

Practice good nutrition.—Eating properly improves overall general health, but under stressful conditions it is even more important. Often tensions and nervous problems are symptoms of poor eating habits.

When stress is compounded by hectic schedules, there is a tendency to consume convenience or overrefined foods that lack significant nutritional benefits. Meals should never be skipped no matter how busy the schedule. Those foods richest in protein, vitamins, and minerals should always be part of the diet (see ch. 5).

Get proper exercise.—Exercise is an ideal way to channel frustration and energy. People in good physical condition can withstand periods of stress, including overwork, quarrels, and depression, better than people who are not.

Fig. 8.3 Eat a well-balanced meal.

Fig. 8.4 Exercise reduces neuromuscular tension.

Exercise relieves neuromuscular tension. Stress at our jobs causes our muscles to tighten and shorten. Muscle construction places stress on the nerves that serve them, and results in neuromuscular tension. Tension can be relieved by participating in vigorous exercise. After strenuous exercise or hard physical labor, muscles are relaxed and the tensions leave your body. Exercise tends to break the vicious stress cycle that we get into each day. So while setting life-style priorities, be sure to include daily time (preferably after work) for favorite activities such as tennis, racquetball, jogging, bicycling, swimming, or walking.

Get proper rest and relaxation.—The final prescription for coping with stress is to allow time for adequate rest and relaxation. We all need sleep time, but also time for just plain relaxing, time to write an overdue letter, or time to put our feet up and let our minds wander.

Research has shown that the best way to relax muscles and nerves is through a progressive relaxation program. This program consists of lying on a firm mat on the floor in a dimly-lighted room with soft music playing. Lie flat on your back with the arms to your side, close your eyes, take deep breaths, and allow your mind to relax all your muscles to the extent there is no movement in your body.

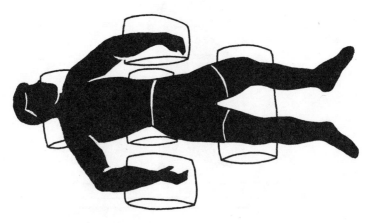

Fig. 8.5 Ideal relaxation position

After you have achieved silence in your nerves and muscles, you are ready to progressively relax each group of muscles in your body. Begin by contracting all the muscles in your legs for five seconds. After the five seconds are over, allow your mind to concentrate on relaxing those muscles. After achieving relaxations in your upper extremities, now contract the muscles in your jaw, eyes, and forehead for five seconds. Then achieve complete relaxation in your head muscles. After achieving relaxation in the head muscles, concentrate on relaxing the whole body for about five minutes. Don't allow any movement to occur to any part of your body. After approximately five minutes, arise, stretch your muscles, and experience how much better you feel.

Achieving complete neuromuscular silence in the nerves and muscles helps eliminate harmful stress. This tension reducing program has proven very successful in reducing stress and tension in hyperactive children. Clearly the words of Isaiah 26:3 still hold: "He will keep in perfect peace all those who trust in him, whose thoughts turn often to the Lord" (TLB).

Alcohol

It is a shame that man did not have the foreknowledge to turn to the Bible for wisdom and instruction concerning the use of alcohol, for God warns many times of the physiological, psychological, economic, social, and moral consequences of drinking alcohol. If man had been obedient to God's Word, think of the lives that could have been saved, the homes that would not have been broken, and all the souls that were lost because of this poisonous chemical compound. Yet, alcohol consumption in the United States is increasing at an alarming rate. An estimated 110 million Americans (over 80 percent of the population) drink alcohol regularly. Statistics reveal that 77 percent of high school students drink alcohol on a regular basis, and that 58 percent of junior high school students now drink routinely. Last year there were 150,000 elementary school-age alcoholics reported in America. Approximately 11

Fig. 8.6 Why not paint the whole picture about alcohol?

million Americans are considered alcoholics. This means that one out of every ten Americans who drink become alcoholics.

Per capita consumption of alcohol is rising. It has risen by 35 percent in the last ten years. Statistically, the average American drinks 2.8 gallons of liquor, 2.7 gallons of wine, and 26.6 gallons of beer annually. Because the alcohol content of each varies, in terms of absolute alcohol; 42 percent comes from hard liquor, 12 percent from wine, and 46 percent from beer. There were roughly 100 cans of beer sold per man, woman, and child in the U.S. I wonder how many glasses of draft beer were sold?

On a worldwide basis, the U.S. has the second highest rate of alcoholism in the world (France ranks first). Among industrial countries, the U.S. currently ranks eighth in per capita consumption of all categories of alcohol, but second in distilled spirits.

The Bible warns against drinking alcohol. "Wine is a

mocker, strong drink a brawler;/and whoever is led astray by it is not wise" (Prov. 20:1, RSV). If we are not wise, then we are stupid. Another translation of Proverbs 20:1 tells us, "It's stupid to get drunk" (GNB). From this scriptural wisdom and from alcohol statistics, we know there are a lot of stupid Americans. Let us analyze our stupidity from drinking alcohol.

The personal cost of alcholism is tremendous. The alcoholic's life expectancy is shortened by ten to twelve years. The mortality rate is two and a half times greater than that of the nondrinker.

Death and injury on the highway due to alcohol have become alarming. According to *Alcohol and Highway Safety Report*, alcohol plays a role in over half of the 50,000 highway deaths each year. In addition, over one million persons are injured, many of them permanently disabled due to alcohol. In other words, more Americans were killed on our highways than were killed in the Vietnam War. Yet no one seems to exhibit much concern over the 28,000 highway deaths from alcohol, unless it is the grieving relatives left behind. Even during the Christmas season when our hearts are full of joy in celebrating Christ's birthday, nearly two thirds of all automobile fatalities are the direct result of alcohol. How long do we intend for this loss of life and limb to continue before we make a concentrated and dedicated effort to stop this needless waste and sorrow?

Alcohol is also reflected in the crime statistics in the U.S. Over half of all homicides and one third of all suicides are alcohol related, resulting in 12,000 deaths a year. Two thirds of all assaults and other felonies are committed by persons under the influence of alcohol. Almost half of the 5.5 million yearly arrested are related to the misuse of alcohol. Alcohol is a universal factor in any family quarrel reported to the police, often resulting in police fatalities. Drunkenness accounts for 1,400,000 arrests yearly. These crimes and misdemeanors cost the taxpayers around $100 million a year in arrest, trial, and jail fees.

The Bible warns that alcohol can lead to poverty. "For the drunkard and the glutton shall come to poverty: and drowsiness shall clothe a man with rags" (Prov. 23:21). American drinkers literally throw away nearly $30 billion annually on alcohol. The same American public, drinker and nondrinker alike, spends nearly the same amount in a futile attempt to repair the damage done by those who drink.

More money is spent on alcoholic beverages (60 billion) than for all educational purposes in this country, two and one-half times as much as for all religious and charitable causes, and several times as much as for all medical and hospital care.

Millions of man hours are lost in industry each year due to the two million alcoholics holding industrial jobs and the millions of dollars in lost pay deprive families of many necessities. A recent survey reported that 41 percent of all welfare and relief checks were cashed in liquor stores. It would be naive to think that some of this money was not taken out in trade.

Drinking alcohol can lead to a life of sadness and poverty. Evangeline Booth, daughter of the founder of the Salvation Army, graphically described the end results of alcohol in these tragic words: "Drink has drained more blood, sold more homes, plunged more people into bankruptcy, armed more villians, slain more children, snapped more wedding rings, defiled more innocence, blinded more eyes, twisted more limbs, dethroned more reason, wrecked more manhood, dishonored more womanhood, broken more hearts, blasted more lives, driven more to suicide, and dug more graves than any other poisonous scourge that ever swept its death-dealing ways across the world." God's Word was right when it says that it is stupid to drink alcohol.

Physiological Effects of Alcohol

One of the most graphic descriptions of the effects of alcohol was written almost 3,000 years ago by King Solomon:

> Who has woe? Who has sorrow?
>   Who has strife? Who has complaining?
> Who has wounds without cause?
>   Who has redness of eyes?

Those who tarry long over wine,
  those who go to try mixed wine.
Do not look at wine when it is red.
  when it sparkles in the cup
  and goes down smoothly.
At the last it bites like a serpent,
  and strings like an adder.
Your eyes will see strange things,
  and your mind utter perverse things.
You will be like one who lies down in the midst
    of the sea,
  like one who lies on the top of a mast.
"They struck me," you will say, "but I was
    not hurt;
  they beat me, but I did not feel it.
When shall I awake?
  I will seek another drink" (Prov. 23:29-35, RSV).

If you are just beginning to drink alcohol or if you only drink in moderation, notice these effects of alcohol on the body. If you are a heavy drinker, please seek professional help for quitting.

Digestive system.—Alcohol is an irritant. This explains the burning sensation as it goes down the digestive tube. To illustrate this irritation, break an egg into a bowl filled with whiskey. The alcohol has enough irritants to cook the egg. Can you imagine what alcohol will do to the delicate mucous membrane lining the digestive system? This may explain the fact that drinkers have more ulcers than nondrinkers. Chronic use of alcohol can cause bleeding, inflammation, loss of appetite, diarrhea, and vomiting. Alcohol frequently causes acute inflammation of the pancreas, which interferes with production of insulin and results in diabetes.

Circulatory system.—Chronic use of alcohol adversely affects the circulatory system. The most common problem is anemia or too few red blood cells, which cannot be manufactured if the bone marrow does not have the necessary ingredients from food intake. Iron is the key ingredient. Alcohol is thought to inhibit the bone marrow's ability to use iron in making hemoglobin, the oxygen-carrying part of the blood.

Chronic use of alcohol also affects white blood cells, the body's main defense against infection. This contributes to increased susceptibility to and frequency of severe infections, especially respiratory tract infections.

Alcohol is thought to be directly responsible for *alcoholic cardiomyopathy*, a specific but uncommon form of heart disease. This condition causes heart failure, shortness of breath at the least exertion, and dramatic enlargement of the heart. Discontinuation of alcohol helps cure this disease.

Alcohol causes abnormalities in cardiac rhythm. Alcohol causes an increase in the frequency of premature ventricular contractions (PVC's). Alcohol, even in moderate amounts, increases the blood fats which increases the rate and development of arteriosclerosis.

Research has shown a definite link between heavy drinking and hypertension. A newly reported alcohol-related heart syndrome, *holiday heart,* occurs after heavy alcohol intake, especially around holidays and on Mondays after weekend binges. The syndrome includes palpitations and arrhythmias but no evidence of cardiomyopathy or congestive heart failure. The signs and symptoms clear completely after a few days of abstinence.

Kidneys.—Anyone who has had a couple of drinks may well spend some time traipsing back and forth to the bathroom. This increased urine output is related to the effect of alcohol on the pituitary gland housed in the brain, not by alcohol's direct action on the kidneys or the amount of liquid consumed. The pituitary secretes a hormone regulating the amount of urine produced. Because the pituitary is adversely affected by alcohol, too little of the hormone is released, and the kidneys form excessive urine. This effect is most pronounced on a rising blood alcohol level while the alcohol is still being absorbed.

Another consequence of chronic alcohol abuse is *hepatorenal syndrome.* This is thought to be caused by a toxic serum factor, or factors, secondary to severe liver disease. These factors cause shifts in kidney blood flow and diminish effective perfusion or filtering through the kidney. Unless the underlying liver disease is somewhat reversed, kidney failure can result.

Liver.—One important role of the liver is to maintain a proper blood sugar level. Sugar (the body's variety, not table sugar) is the only source of energy the brain cells use. Because the brain is the master control center of the body, an inadequate supply of food has far-reaching consequences. When alcohol is present, the liver gives its whole attention to metabolizing the alcohol and does not manufacture and release glucose (sugar) into the bloodstream, thus creating a drop in blood sugar. This is a hypoglycemic state—a below normal concentration of blood sugar. The brain is deprived of proper nourishment. Symptoms include hunger, weakness, nervousness, sweating, headache, and tremor. If the level is sufficiently depressed, coma can occur.

Reproductive system.—Heavy alcohol use affects the reproductive system by causing skipped menstrual period in women and sterility in men. Although sexual interests and pursuits may be heightened by alcohol's release of inhibitions, ability to perform sexually can be impaired. For example, men may be either relatively or absolutely impotent.

Alcohol and pregnancy.—Pregnant women should not drink alcohol, even in so-called "moderation," for serious consequences could occur to the body. Drinking alcohol while pregnant can cause *fetal alcohol syndrome.* Alcohol passes through the placenta to the developing fetus and interferes with prenatal development. At birth, infants with fetal alcohol syndrome are smaller, both in weight and length. Head size and brain growth decrease. At birth, infants are jittery and tremulous. Whether this jitteriness is the result of nervous system impairment from the long-term exposure to alcohol or from mini withdrawal is unclear. There have been reports of newborn infants having the scent of alcohol on their first breath. Cardiac problems and retardation are also associated with this syndrome. This syndrome is now the third leading cause of mental retardation. In fact, 74 percent of all malformed children are born to drinking mothers. I read a bumper sticker that sums up everything and gives us something to think about: "Pregnant women never drink alone."

If drinking alcohol is so bad for you, then why do so many Christians drink? There are a number of possible reasons, none of which is sufficiently compelling to justify the end result.

One reason is the social pressure to conform. You are just not "in" unless you drink. Another reason is the attractive advertisements that are portrayed through the media: the successful business person, the great athlete, surrounded by expensive cars and luxurious mansions. The liquor companies should show pictures of the end results—the alcoholics, the bums, the prostitutes, the victims of car wrecks, the stabbings and shootings, the broken homes, the orphans, the brokenhearted and disgraced parents, the diseased minds and bodies, the poverty, and the ruined lives.

Another reason why Christians drink is to escape from reality. Most experts agree that most people drink to escape the realities of life than for any other reason. Alcohol undoubtedly provides an effective escape mechanism, resulting often in complete oblivion to the problems and unpleasant realities of everyday living. However, no one has ever used alcohol for this purpose without awakening to the realization that the original problem is no better and is probably worse.

Most teenagers drink because their parents do. In fact, the majority of these young people probably had their first experience with beverage alcohol at home, usually at age thirteen or fourteen. Studies indicate that by the time teenagers graduate from high school, virtually all of them have at least experimented with alcoholic beverages. Other studies reveal that four out of five teenagers believe that drinking is right and acceptable under certain circumstances. Only one in five thought that drinking was unequivocally wrong.

We as Christian parents should teach our children at home

the dangers of alcohol and the principles of life and Christian living that will lead them to turn away from alcohol. Our schools and churches can exert little influence in this direction unless we as adults are willing to lead the way, both in precept and example. As parents we can seek to provide a well-adjusted and secure home environment in which our children may grow and learn and develop. We can set the proper example for moral and disciplined living.

Finally, an honest recognition of our responsibility to God to care for our bodies should be the greatest deterrent to the use of alcoholic beverages. When we degrade our bodies, we bring disgrace to our Creator in whose image we have been made.

Smoking Tobacco

The surgeon general of the United States now has over thirty thousand studies to back up his mandate which was issued in 1964, that "smoking is hazardous to your health." Yet, the department of Health, Education, and Welfare figures indicate that about one third of the nation's population still smoke. Even more alarming is the fact that every two minutes, some five teenagers begin smoking. In fact, there is an almost 50 percent increase in smoking in teenage girls. If teenagers become habitual smokers, they will shorten their lives by an average of six minutes for each cigarette they smoke. Statistics indicate that smokers die nearly nine years sooner than non-smokers.

This significant use of tobacco in America is rather remarkable in view of the overwhelming evidence that tobacco smoke is both poisonous and irritating to the body and its various delicate tissues. Table 8.2 reveals some of the known poisonous substances that have been isolated from tobacco smoke.

Nicotine is one of the most rapid and fatal of poisons. One pack of cigarettes contains an amount of nicotine which, if given in a single injection, would almost certainly kill a per-

Table 8.2 Poisonous Substances Found in Cigarette Smoke

Substance	Substance as it is used in our society
1. hydrogen cyanide	used to execute criminals in gas chambers
2. carbon monoxide	gas used to commit suicide (car exhaust)
3. arsenious oxide	used to murder people (form of arsenic)
4. formaldehyde	used to embalm people
5. ammonia	I use it to clean my toilet
6. nicotine	used as an insecticide for crops

son. What makes this poison even worse is that it is physiologically addictive. It is the body, not the psyche, that cries loudest when smokers try to stop. According to medical researchers, nicotine reaches the brain within a few minutes after the first drag. But within twenty to thirty minutes (precisely the time lag between cigarettes for most heavy smokers), the nicotine has dissipated to other organs, and another cigarette is needed.

The health consequences of smoking tobacco are numerous. Our research libraries are filled with studies that link smoking to various diseases. Smoking has been found to cause cancer of the lips, larynx, trachea, bronchial tree, and lungs. It has been found to cause emphysema, which probably causes the most suffering of all diseases. People with emphysema have to breathe over 100,000 times a day, and each breath bring severe pain. I do not think God created our respiratory systems to function in this terrifying manner. Don't smoke!

Circulatory disorders are found far more frequently in smokers than in nonsmokers. The gas exchange in the lungs (alveoli) is not as efficient, which means that the heart is required to pump a greater amount of blood through the lungs for a given saturation level of hemoglobin with oxygen. It also means a faster-breathing rate.

One circulatory disorder is Buerger's disease. Nicotine apparently causes constriction of the arterioles (small arteries) of the extremities so that circulation is seriously impaired. Gangrene, amputation, and, ultimately, death result. I met a man who had both legs amputated because of Buerger's disease. He had a cigarette dangling from his lips, and when I questioned him about why he hadn't quit smoking, his reply was, "I like the taste."

Coronary thrombosis (heart attack) occurs three times as frequently in men who smoke more than one pack of cigarettes a day as opposed to nonsmokers. This observation is related to the influence of nicotine on cholestrol metabolism. Research shows that free fatty acids in the bloodstream rise about 25 percent in the normal persons after smoking but increase up to 65 percent in patients with coronary artery disease. It has been estimated that death and illness due to heart attacks could be reduced by almost one half if all smokers gave up this senseless habit.

Overwhelming evidence indicates that maternal smoking during pregnancy affects fetal growth. Babies born to women who smoke during pregnancy are, on the average, a half pound lighter than babies born to nonsmoking mothers. The premature birth rate for mothers who smoke is two-and-one-half the rate for nonsmokers. The miscarriage rate for smokers is about 50 percent higher than for those who did not smoke. Maternal smoking can be a direct cause of fetal or neonatal death in an otherwise normal infant. The immediate cause of most smoking-related fetal deaths is probably anoxia (lack of oxygen) which can be attributed to placental complications with antepartum bleeding in 30 percent or more of the cases.

In summary, the death rate for those who smoke is about twice as high as for those who do not. On the basis of these statistics and the associated health consequences, there seems to be no logical justification whatsoever for the use of tobacco, especially in the form of cigarettes.

Exposure of nonsmokers to tobacco smoke.—The smoke inhaled by the cigarette smoker is termed the mainstream smoke; that which trails off the end of the cigarette is the sidestream smoke. Sidestream smoke represents about 50 percent of the tobacco burned, and is responsible for approximately

Fig. 8.7 Nonsmokers should have rights.

two thirds of the aerosol particles delivered to the environment. Sidestream smoke has higher concentrations of the irritating and hazardous substances. Cigarette smoking in enclosed spaces can produce carbon monoxide levels well above the surrounding air quality (nine parts per million) even when ventilation is adequate. The Surgeon General's Report found that the levels of carbon monoxide in cigarette-filled environments decrease the exercise duration required to induce angina pectoris (heart pain) in patients with coronary artery disease. These carbon monoxide levels also reduce the exercise time until onset dyspnea (difficulty in breathing) in patients with hypotic chronic lung disease. Children of parents who smoke are more likely to have bronchitis and pneumonia during the first year of life.

The smoker hurts not only himself but also can damage the health of those around. Also, many other aspects are offensive to others. The smoker who blows fumes into the face of another person, or flicks ashes on a rug, or grinds a cigarette butt into the floor is most rude and inconsiderate. The smoker who burns hundreds of thousands of acres of forest land by the careless flip of a lighted cigarette out a car window can cause just as much damage as the arsonist. The vast majority of forest fires are thought to be caused by careless smokers. It has been estimated that one out of every six serious fires in homes and hotels is caused by cigarettes. There is no rational way in which to justify the use of such a lethal object. I hope you join an antismoking group and continually support ways and means of helping people stop smoking.

If smoking is such a dangerous habit, why do approximately seventy million Americans engage in this practice? One reason is that nicotine is a strongly addicting drug. Nicotine is sought for its pharmacological effect on the central nervous system. Pleasurable effects are felt almost immediately upon inhalation. Smokers describe the effects as both stimulating and relaxing, and almost always as relieving a craving. The conclusion is that nicotine is a strongly addictive substance to which dependency can develop in a short time, most often leading to a lifelong habit. Much harm is done by leading young people to believe that they can smoke for a few years and then quit.

Most cigarette smokers do not need medical evidence to tell them that the habit is harmful. They tend to minimize the effects, however, and hold the rather fatalistic belief that the gravest consequences will befall someone else. Research has determined that cigarette smoking is harmful to virtually all persons who indulge in it, and the effects are cumulative. The longer and more intense the habit, the graver the effect. Many of the pathological changes are reversible when the habit is broken. More cutting down or smoking cigarettes with special filters is usually of little benefit. Cigar and pipe smokers show higher mortality rate for chronic bronchitis and emphysema than nonsmokers, but these rates are not as great as for cigarette smokers.

The majority of cigarette smokers who have tried to quit have succeeded in varying degrees. Withdrawal symptoms are real, and for many, intolerable. Probably most effective is the one-day-at-a-time method. Resolve to have no cigarette today and let tomorrow take care of itself.

Smoking, like drinking, overeating, and drug dependence, is a form of lust that can be conquered with a combination of stamina and God. Your discipline, motivation, and commitment joined with God's support, wisdom, and strength will make an unconquerable team. Your part is to "make not provision for the flesh, to fulfil the lusts thereof" (Rom. 13:14). God's part is committed in his promise of spiritual power: "Walk in the Spirit, and ye shall not fulfil the lust of the flesh" (Gal. 5:16).

Smoking Marijuana

Marijuana? Where don't you find it today? From the slums to the Congress the weed has spread until it has become a national habit. Sometime today, a couple of million Americans will light up cigarettes hand rolled from dried marijuana leaves, popularly known as joints of pot, grass, or Mary Jane. An estimated 50 million Americans have tried marijuana at some time, and 16 million are current users. Most of our country's pot smokers are young; only 7 percent of those over thirty-five have tried the drug. Among those eighteen to twenty-five years of age, one in four currently uses it, and three out of five have tried it one or more times.

What is it? Marijuana is made from the dried leaves of the plant *Cannabis sativa. Cannabis* is hardy and plentiful and thrives in virtually every country of the world. It contains an intoxicating drug called tetrahydrocannabinol (THC). The THC content of the cannabis plant varies, with the strongest concentrations found in the resin (hashish) and lesser amounts in the flowers and leaves.

Unlike most drugs, smoking marijuana affects God's temple in three ways. First, it has an intoxicating effect approximately equal to that of alcohol. Smoking one joint can reduce reaction time by 41 percent. Can you imagine a pot smoker driving an automobile while intoxicated with THC?

Second, marijuana has a hallucinogenic effect on the body similar to LSD or PCP. It causes some individuals to see and hear imaginary things. Many think they are a bird and can fly off tall buildings.

Third, it has a sedative effect like barbiturates. After the high, many experience depression. Researchers are inclined to categorize marijuana as unique, in a class by itself. The principal psychoactive chemical, THC, is one of sixty-one cannabinoids and other substances found in marijuana that may have a direct effect on mental and physical functions.

THC remains in the fatty tissues of every cell, especially in the brain and gonads, many days after smoking just one joint. Even a week later, 30 to 50 percent of the THC is still in the body in active form. Having this poison in God's cells interferes with the normal functions of the cell, and causes this marvelously created masterpiece to be less than God intends it to be.

Effect on the brain.—Pot has an affinity for the brain as well as the sex organs. Marijuana's sixty-one cannabinoids are soluble in fat. They are attracted to the body's fatty organs, where they remain, only gradually released from the body. Radioactivity has been used to trace THC in the body, and it takes five to eight days for just half the THC in a single marijuana cigarette to clear from the body. In fact, traces of THC can be found in the body for six weeks after smoking it.

The human brain contains a large amount of fat cells called glia cells. From observations in animal studies, marijuana buildup causes brain cells to show striking structural changes, including abnormal deposits of opaque material in the synaptic cleft between neurons. This interferes with the chemical process of the synapes and causes a slowing down or interruption in the movement of brain messages. An abnormal clumping of the small sacs in the endings of nerve cells that contain the chemical activators of the brain was also found, plus a significant increase of foreign matter in the nerve cell nuclei. All of these conditions are associated with brain impair-

173

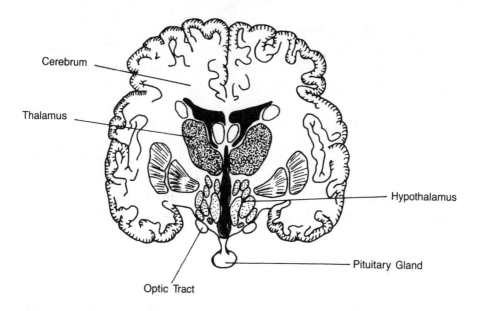

Fig. 8.8 Pituitary gland in brain

ment and can cause a loss of memory, reverse *d*'s and *b*'s in handwriting, and abnormal electroencephalogram (EEG) recordings. For example, a concerned mother asked me to counsel with her son who had smoked marijuana for two years. He couldn't even remember his sister's name, much less remember his childhood experiences.

A prominent physician represents the findings of many drug therapists when he says: "Most of the time, when kids stop smoking pot, they will regain what short-term memory they have lost. But I've also seen cases of kids, who were chronic users, or who combined pot with another drug (usually alcohol) where there was no subsequent improvement."[1]

Effect on sex.—As little as a billionth of a gram of THC affects the hypothalamus, which in turn, affects the pituitary gland, which regulates endocrine function and the hormones controlling sex and reproduction.

A study conducted by Masters and Johnson Institute found that 31 percent of the menstrual cycles of pot-smoking women showed a shortened luteal phase, which could mean

174

that a growing embryo might not be properly nourished. These women also had decreased prolactin, a hormone important in milk production.

A survey of 500 men, ages eighteen to thirty, who had smoked pot for six or seven years, showed statistically significant lower rates of sexual activity and fewer orgasms. The survey also revealed that 20 percent of the male patients who had smoked for five or more years complained of impotence. Other studies indicate that cannabinoids result in lower sperm count and in a larger number of abnormally shaped sperm.

Pot smoking may also affect unborn children. A human female is born with about 400,000 eggs. If injured, the eggs cannot be repaired. Radioactivity tagging of THC shows that it accumulates in the ovaries as well as in other organs. Controlled animal studies have found that THC caused death in nearly half of the eggs in female animals. Of those that had lived, 20 to 30 percent looked unhealthy.

In an animal study, THC mothers produced dead or dying offspring in 44 percent of their offspring compared with 12 percent in a control group. Although all of the dead babies of the THC drugged animals looked normal, microscopic evaluation of tissues and organs showed subtle developmental abnormalities in various tissues and organ systems of the THC

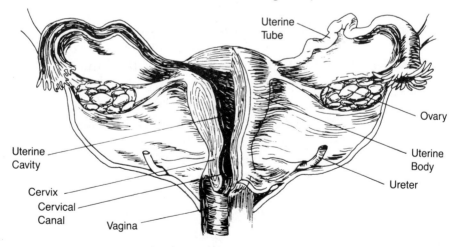

Fig. 8.9 Female reproductive system

offspring that were not present in the dead offspring of the undrugged mothers.

The sperm, egg, and fetus must be regarded as sources of possible congenital damage in surviving offspring. THC diminishes the capacity of individual cells to orchestrate life according to the genetic plan God built into cellular molecules. THC inhibits formation of DNA in cells, resulting in cellular death and abnormality.

Some pot smokers discount findings (especially on animals) about marijuana's possible genetic effects, but until all definite findings are in, pregnant marijuana smokers should heed the present warning signals. The former director of the National Institute on Drug Abuse puts it this way: "Our youngsters are, in effect, making themselves guinea pigs in a tragic national experiment. Thus far, our research clearly suggests that you will see horrendous results."

Don't play genetic roulette by smoking marijuana. I can think of no sadder experience than for a young couple to experience the birth of a malformed child because of their foolishness. Out bodies constitute the very dwelling place of the Spirit of God. Be your best by keeping God's house clean.

Cocaine

$C_{17} H_{21} NO_4$, otherwise known as cocaine, coke, C, snow, or blow. An alkaloid derived from the leaves of the coca plant. One can purchase it almost anywhere in the United States. The cost is $2,200 per ounce, or about five times the price of gold. Whatever the price, by whatever the name, cocaine is becoming the all-American drug. No longer is it just an exotic indulgence of Hollywood types and high rollers. Today, in part because it is seen as an emblem of wealth and status, cocaine is the drug of choice for millions of otherwise conventional citizens.

Some researchers estimate that fifteen million Americans now use cocaine with some regularity, and another ten million have probably experimented with it. According to a 1982 survey by the National Institute on Drug Abuse, about 32 percent of young adults eighteen to twenty-five years old reported that they had used cocaine. In 1977, only 19 percent said they had tried the drug.

Effect on the body.—American drug laws classify cocaine as a narcotic, along with opium, heroin, and morphine. But these last three are depressants ("downers"), drugs that quiet the body and dull the senses, while coke is a stimulant, or "upper," similar to amphetamines. It increases the heart rate, raises blood pressure and body temperature, and curbs appetite. Like a shot of adrenalin, cocaine puts the body into an emergency state.

Like any other stimulant, cocaine influences the action of the body chemicals called neurotransmitters. These chemicals fire off one nerve cell after another like a string of firecrackers, sending tiny electrical impulses coursing through the nervous system. As the signals multiply, they inundate the areas of the system that control such involuntary functions as pulse and perspiration. They also flood at least two critical parts of the brain itself: the cerebral cortex, which governs higher mental activities like memory and reasoning, and the hypothalamus (appetite, body temperature, and sleep, as well as such emotions as anger and fear).

The brain becomes like an overburdened telephone switchboard. It cannot handle all the messages. There is too much information flowing in, and the user becomes hyper-aroused. With larger doses and chronic use, the alertness and exhilaration, so prized by cocaine connoisseurs, quickly turn into darker effects, ranging from insomnia to psychosis. The drug may also increase the risk of heart attacks, especially among those with cardiac problems. Even a single overdose can cause severe headaches, nausea, convulsions, and maybe total respiratory and cardiovascular collapse.

Most cocaine users sniff the white powder through the nose, ensuring absorption into the bloodstream through the mucous membranes. Sniffing also constricts the myriad little blood vessels in these membranes, reduces the blood supply, and dries up the nose. With repeated coke use, ulcers form, cartilage is exposed, and the nasal septum can become perforated, requiring surgical repair.

Equally disturbing is the fact that cocaine is the most psychologically tenacious drug available. Coming down from a high may cause such deep depression that the only remedy is more cocaine. Bigger doses often follow, and soon the urge may become a total obsession, with all its devastating consequences.

Another phenomenon which cocaine users also experience is formication. This is the feeling that ants, insects, or snakes are crawling under or on one's skin. With the user in such a state, the possibility of violence cannot be discounted.

Christian happiness is not found in a bottle of alcohol or from a lighted cigarette. It is not found in some drug that may stimulate the body's senses for a short period of time. Happiness comes when we follow God's teachings to the best of our ability. I find it hard to believe that God would condone the use of such destructive habits that destroys his wonderful creation. His Word teaches to the contrary. To really experience the "abundant life" promised in John, become the best servant of God possible. This includes taking care of his temple to the best of your ability.

Note

1. G. Andrews and S. Vinkenoog, *The Book of Grass: An Anthology of Indian Hymns* (New York: Grove Press, 1967).

CHAPTER 9

Happiness Comes from Being Self-Controlled

For God did not give us a spirit of timidity but a spirit of power and love and self-control"

(2 Tim. 1:7, RSV).

The reason for long countdowns prior to spacecraft liftoffs is to get everything under control. The guidance system with all its scientific checks and counterbalances must be in order. If a spacecraft is to reach its destiny, a great deal of care must be given to the guidance system. This is the case with humans, too, yet many Christians choose to live at full speed without any regard for traffic signals or road maps.

The writer of Proverbs issued a solemn warning on this point. "A man without self-control is like a city broken into and left without walls" (Prov. 25:28, RSV). In ancient times a city could not exist long without walls and fortifications. Such a city could be sacked and destroyed. Any person who is unable to control his own life is in the same precarious situation.

If you don't care what happens to yourself or what you become, who do you suppose will care? Who really should care, if you don't?

The Principle of Self-Control

The free-wheeling life sooner or later self-destructs. Disregard for the physical needs of the body soon brings despair. We are surrounded by the temptations of Satan and by our own inner weaknesses. Unless we determine to "exercise self-control" we will find ourselves in the grip of the powers of darkness. The quality and future of our life is at stake. Self-control will determine whether we will look back on our life rejoicing or cursing the day of our birth.

Fig. 9.1 "I do not box as one beating the air."

The apostle Paul was the greatest missionary ever. On one occasion he shared his secret for being able to accomplish so much. "Well, I do not run aimlessly, I do not box as one beating the air; but I pommel my body and subdue it, lest after preaching to others I myself should be disqualified" (1 Cor. 9:26-27, RSV). He realized that he could ruin his future, his usefulness in the kingdom of God, if he failed to rule his own body and spirit well. If he wanted to do the best things in life, there were some lesser things he could not afford to become involved in.

Paul used the world of athletics to speak of the necessary discipline needed for achieving his own personal goals. He noted that everyone in a race should run in an effort to win, and that everyone who wants to master any sport must be serious about it, must pay the price of training.

Fig. 9.2 "I run a race to win."

Anyone who takes Christianity seriously, who tries to live the godly life, must recognize that such a task is not easy. The truth is, those who dare to follow Christ may find that many things do not always go better. To follow Christ is sometimes to travel upstream or to go against the tide. If life with Christ were the easy life, everyone would follow him. However, the good life is a difficult, yet rewarding life. Only those who are willing to rule their own body and spirit, to exercise self-control and discipline, can live it.

The person you become is directly related to whether or not you choose to exercise self-control over your life. Paul expressed his philosophy on this matter in 1 Corinthians when he wrote, "All things are lawful unto me, but all things are not expedient: all things are lawful for me, but I will not be brought under the power of any" (6:12). The apostle refused to become a slave to anything, including bad habits and evil temptations. He refused to be a part of anything that was not expedient (made a contribution), or was enslaving.

Your personality develops only on the same ratio with which you grow in maturity. Maturity is a willingness to postpone fulfillment of present desires; and self-control governs the growth of maturity. People either learns to rule their own lives, to control themselves, or they take into their life everything that presents itself.

You will never discover the real you, never grow to be your unique self, until you are willing to exercise self-control. We can have more than human strength to rule our spirit with, for our Heavenly Father will give us so much strength as we allow him to. The Christian life is the self-controlled life, guided and empowered by Christ. We can say with the apostle Paul, "I can do all things through Christ which strengtheneth me" (Phil. 4:13). The apostle also said in the same letter: "Being confident of this very thing, that he which hath begun a good work in you will perform it until the day of Jesus Christ" (Phil. 1:6).

For many of us to be happy, we may need to develop whole new life-styles. We need to make a new commitment to God that we want to serve him the best that we can. This means we must "seek first his kingdom and his righteousness" in every facet of our lives (Matt. 6:33, RSV). This means we must also try to love our neighbor as ourselves (Matt. 22:39). And finally, we must practice self-control over our lives by showing honor and glory to God with our bodies (1 Cor. 6:20). Only when we are in excellent physical condition can we serve him the best that we can.

You Can

I shared an office with a colleague and friend who had a sign displayed on our office wall which read in large letters "You Can." I can't begin to tell you how that sign has changed many facets of my life. Every time I'm faced with a new challenge in my busy schedule, I immediately respond with excuses and rationalizations that I cannot possibly accept this new challenge. Then I look at that sign hanging on the wall and confidence overshadows my laziness. The point is, "You Can."

You can start an exercise program at any age. There are thousands of senior adults who can testify to that statement. Recently a senior adult woman came up to me after a fitness seminar and remarked: "Look at me, I'm so old I can *barely* walk. How can I start exercising?" My response to her question was "Then start *barely* walking." Two years later I received a letter from her with these responses: "I took your advice about walking. I'm now walking three miles a day. I feel better; my body is getting stronger; I can do more work for God. By the way, I won three people to Christ on my eighty-eighth birthday."

That is the "bottom line" of why we should exercise and take care of God's temple to the best of our ability. So we can serve him longer and better. The Bible doesn't say that we are not to witness after we reach sixty-five years of age. We, as Christians, have the responsibility to serve God from our first breath to our last. May each of us strengthen our body through exercising so that we can become a better servant for him.

Many Christians use excuses such as "I'm too handicapped by some physical malady to begin an exercise program." Let me share an experience of the most courageous accomplishment I have ever witnessed in a sporting event. After completing a marathon run of twenty-six miles, 385 yards in my record time, I decided to watch other runners finish the marathon course. After watching for about five minutes, I saw the crowd giving a standing ovation to a pair of runners and sensed an emotion so strong that chill bumps covered my body and tears came to my eyes. For you see, these runners had run stride for stride twenty-six miles, 385 yards together with unbelievable handicaps. The lead runner's feet were amputated at the ankle joint and he had to run on a wooden prosthesis. He held a rope in his hand and running behind him was the other runner holding the rope, who was completely blind. I looked at the pride of those runners crossing that finish line and again the words of that sign in my office entered my mind.

Christian, *you can* begin an exercise program even though you have a handicap. As a little child once said, "God didn't create no junk." Your body may now be in poor physical condition, but through a slow, progressive exercise program you can build it up and improve its efficiency. The only real excuse for not exercising is laziness. Many Christians don't want to put forth the effort it takes to strengthen the temple. Don't be lazy. Make a lifetime commitment to physical fitness and enjoy some of life's happy fulfillments.

The Ideal Physical Fitness Program

The exercise program given in table 9.1 was developed from personal experience and is based on the latest research. To attain maximal benefits from exercise, it is essential to plan a progressive program that meets your specific needs. The following suggestions can help form your exercise program.

Identify your own fitness needs.—The main health related components of physical fitness are cardiovascular-respiratory (CVR) fitness, muscular strength and endurance fitness, flexibility fitness, and body composition fitness. You may have developed fitness in strength but may have neglected flexibility fitness. Check your fitness level in each of these four areas by reading the appropriate chapters and self-testing yourself. Now select a mode of training that can best improve your weakest areas.

Select a program that meets all of your fitness needs.—Marathon runners are not always physically fit, because they may lack sufficient strength in their upper body which could lead to postural deviations. No single exercise can meet all of your needs. Select exercises in all aspects of physical fitness and especially make sure you have selected a program you enjoy. If you do not enjoy it, you may not carry it through to a meaningful result.

Select a regular time and place for your exercise.—Begin your workouts at approximately the same time every day. Try not to allow any outside influence to interfere with this precious time. You may want to exercise at different places. It is fun to vary the route if you walk or jog. Set a goal for yourself. Great satisfaction comes from reaching that goal. Record your progress on a chart. Build your exercise program into your daily routine and make it as much a habit as combing your hair or brushing your teeth.

Do not overexercise.—This can cause soreness or uncomfortable pain which will cause you to terminate your exercise program. Approach each exercise program with a positive attitude. Be thankful you are able to exercise.

Warm up and cool down before and after each exercise workout.—Approximately two minutes of easy jogging or three minutes of walking should precede an exercise bout to improve blood flow to the heart and muscles. Static stretching of the muscles prior to exercise can also reduce soreness and possible injury.

Cooling down or slowly tapering off after exercise is advisable. Never stop exercising abruptly. After a jog or a bout of exercise, continue to walk and move around.

The ideal exercise program (table 9.1) develops all the health-related components of fitness. It strengthens the muscles and their various movements in a balanced manner. It also builds up flexibility in the joints and muscles but, more importantly, it develops a sufficient amount of CVR fitness. This program also allows for individual differences in fitness by permitting each person to develop at his own intensity, no matter what age or fitness level. For example, the highly fit person can train his CVR system (run, swim, bicycle, etc.) at an intensity level high enough to meet his needs. He may be able to run seven to eight miles in forty minutes, whereas the unfit individual may be able to cover only two to three miles in forty minutes. The key is to exercise at a pace that meets the requirements of the 60 to 70 percent intensity level for thirty to forty minutes. Fitness in each of these physical fitness components will definitely improve God's temple which will be pleasing to you and show honor and glory to him.

Table 9.1 An Ideal Exercise Program

Monday	1. Do 5 minutes of flexibility exercises described in chapter 7 before and after workout.
	2. Select your favorite mode of CVR exercise (walking, jogging, bicycling, swimming, aerobic dance) and perform for 30-40 minutes. Try to keep your working heart rate at the desired intensity level (60-70 percent) while exercising. (See ch. 4.)
Tuesday	1. Do 5 minutes of flexibility exercises before and after workout.
	2. Do 20-30 minutes of CVR training.
	3. Do strength training exercises for each body movement as described in chapter 6. Make sure you work each muscle at every major joint equally.
Wednesday	Repeat Monday's schedule.
Thursday	Repeat Tuesday's schedule.
Friday	Repeat Monday and Wednesday's schedule.
Saturday	Repeat Tuesday and Thursday's schedule.
Sunday	Day of rest. Go to church.

This exercise program usually takes between forty-five minutes to an hour to complete each day. By the end of six weeks you will definitely notice and feel a change in your body's physiology. Motivate yourself to stay with the program for at least six weeks and by then you will definitely believe that exercise should be a part of your life-style.

We need to develop our lives as Jesus did. We need to develop our potential mentally, socially, spiritually, and physically. We should never neglect any one of these areas of potential growth, for complications will occur in other areas.

The Bible tells us that we are the body of Christ. We are

what Jesus left on earth. He left us to represent him to the world. His Spirit has come to dwell within us, and the world will know our God mainly by our representation of him, which will be greatly enhanced if we develop fully this potential that he has created in us. Do not be lazy, or use excuses like age, lack of time, or "I'm too busy," to develop these four areas of growth. God wants you to be happy and have the abundant life. He knows the only way for you to achieve this is for you to develop the unlimited potential that he has given you. Striving to achieve this potential will help you serve him better and help you become a happy person.

My prayer for you is beautifully expressed by the apostle John in his Third Epistle. "I wish above all things that thou mayest prosper and be in health, even as thy soul prospereth" (v. 2).

Notes

1. Kenneth Cooper, *The New Aerobics* (New York: Bantam Books, 1970).
2. B. Getchell, *Physical Fitness: A Way of Life* (New York: John Wiley and Sons).

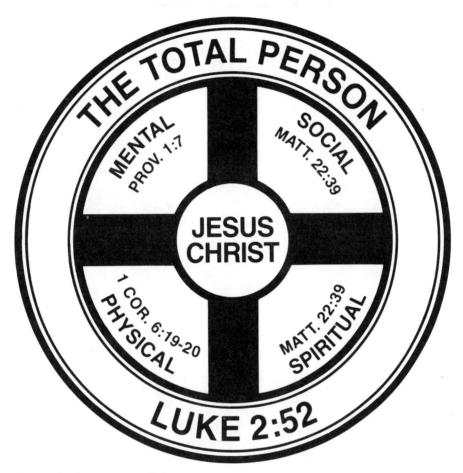

Fig. 9.3   Develop in all areas.